PREVENTING DROPOUT AND OVERCOMING SCHOOL FAILURE

30 Ways for Older Teens and Young Adults to Achieve Academic Success

ISRAELIN SHOCKNESS

Successful Youth Living - Vol. 4

Copyright © 2017, 2020 by Israelin Shockness.

Vanquest Publishing Inc.

Requests for information can be obtained by contacting Info@SuccessfulYouthLiving.com

Cataloguing-in-Publication Data

Israelin Shockness

Includes bibliographical references

PREVENTING DROPOUT AND OVERCOMING SCHOOL FAILURE

30 Ways for Older Teens and Young Adults to Achieve Academic Success - Vol. 4 (2nd Ed.)

ISBN: 978-1-989480-02-1 (paperback)

ISBN: 978-1-989480-03-8 (ebook)

SERIES – Successful Youth Living - Vol. 4 (2nd Ed.)

All rights reserved. No part of this publication may be reproduced, stored in a retrieval system, or transmitted in any form or by any means – electronic, mechanical, photocopy, recording, or any other – except for brief quotations in printed reviews, without the prior permission of the author (Info@IsraelinShockness.com).

Disclaimer

All materials provided in this book are for information purposes only and should not be taken as a substitute for professional, psychological, or mental health advice. It is intended to encourage and motivate you to think and to have meaningful conversations around these issues, the objective being to promote more responsible behavior at all times. If, for any reason, you feel you are experiencing any emotional or other crisis, you are encouraged to seek out professional care. References have been made to peer-reviewed and other research studies and works, but this is not intended to imply specific endorsement of this author's work by any of these authors and professionals mentioned. Any incorrect attribution of ideas to an author was not intentional and will be corrected at earliest possibility. The opinions expressed in this book are solely those of this author and not those of the publisher. Further, the publisher is exempt from any responsibility for actions taken by the reader with respect to the content and acknowledges that the reader acts of their own accord in using information presented and holds the author and the publisher blameless in the reader's use of the content.

Purpose of This Series

Successful Youth Living is a series of books, dealing with issues, which older teens and young adults face as they go through the uncertainty of adolescence. A few of the topics dealt with are: becoming a leader in your own right without being a bully; learning how to assume responsibility; fostering positive attitudes and habits for self-growth; learning how to continue your education regardless of where you stopped or whether you dropped out; developing emotional intelligence and caring for self and others; learning how to deal with stress; recognizing the importance of personal reflection; and being a person that others admire for the right reasons.

The 'seed' for these volumes was actually planted when the author, then a teenager on a scholarship, almost dropped out of university because of her inability to deal with many issues that had nothing to do with school. Thanks to the insightfulness and mentorship of a professor, the author became a teen mentor and since then have committed herself to paying it forward by looking out for vulnerable teens and young adults that have lost their way, the way she had almost lost hers. After years of further study, a career as an educator working with children, teens and young adults, years as a volunteer in marginalized communities and as a columnist in a weekly community newspaper, Israelin has recognized that many of the issues plaguing adolescents have not changed. She has therefore decided to share ideas she has gleaned from personal experience, as well as from her students, readers, studies, and from peer-reviewed articles.

DEDICATION

This book is dedicated to teens and youths, to young millennials, as well as to young adults. Going through the transitional stage of adolescence can be a very challenging, and sometimes confusing, one for many. Not only is this a period of many physical changes, but it is also a period of emotional, intellectual, cognitive, and social ones.

With the age of youth extending from the teenage years well into the thirties, many young people are now facing challenges as to when to take on adult roles and how to go about these roles. This "trying on" of adult roles is individual and unique, and presents many challenges for young people of different ages.

This is also a period when many young people face so many challenges that they let some areas of their lives just fall by the wayside. This particularly happens in the area of education. This may happen because some young people may have learning difficulties or because they may have missed some critical periods during their school life. But other young people, because of challenges they may have been experiencing at the time just could not keep up with their education, even though they may have been good students. This experience may have contributed to many young people dropping out of high school or even college or university.

However, this is not usually the end of their concern with their education. For many, there may be a major awakening coming a few years down the road and probably two children later, when these young people realize that they are ill-equipped to earn a living for themselves and for their growing families.

Matters may become more complicated when they realize that they not only have to face the prospect of improving their level of employability, but that they have to face helping their children with homework. These two concerns often cause these young people, who had dropped out of school, to experience anxiety, regret, and disappointment that they did not move further on their educational journey.

Then comes a glimmer of hope, followed by lots of doubt and hopelessness: "I should go back to school, but what should I do?" "I am too old to think about school?" "I cannot learn at this age?" "How embarrassing for me to go back to school at this time of my life." "Too many years have passed since I left school." "Who am I kidding?" "I am not school material," and "What would people say?"

These are some of the sentiments I have heard expressed by young adults, who came face to face with their unpreparedness to enter the job market, and their realization that they needed more education and training. Doubts at this juncture of their lives often led to depression and even more anxiety.

But I am here to tell you that whether you dropped out of school several years ago, whether you recently did so, or whether you are toying with the idea of dropping out of school, all is not lost. There is opportunity for all of you to restart your education. It is my hope that this book will provide some pointers that would help you in moving forward on your educational journey, with the motivation that you can succeed at what you set out to achieve.

After reading this book and implementing some of the strategies mentioned, you are encouraged to share your experiences with us. Let us hear about your successes and let others hear how you did it, so that they, too, would be encouraged and motivated to move ahead.

You can reach us at info@SuccessfulYouthLiving.com.

TABLE OF CONTENTS

CHAPTER 1: BE THE VERY BEST YOU CAN BE 11

CHAPTER 2: THE PORTRAIT OF A GOOD STUDENT 21

CHAPTER 3: "I AM NOT A GOOD STUDENT AND
I HATE SCHOOL" 29

CHAPTER 4: ARE YOU MISSING IN ACTION? 35

CHAPTER 5: SAVING HIGH SCHOOL 43

CHAPTER 6: SKIPPING CLASSES - SKIPPING SCHOOL 51

CHAPTER 7: HAVE YOU ALREADY DROPPED
OUT OF SCHOOL? 59

CHAPTER 8: TAKING THINGS FOR GRANTED? 69

CHAPTER 9: "HOW CAN I MAKE THIS WORK?" 75

CHAPTER 10: ARE YOU SABOTAGING YOUR
COMPREHENSION 83

CHAPTER 11: LEARNING DISABILITY AND
SLEEP DEPRIVATION 89

CHAPTER 12: SO WHAT IF YOU ARE 'SLOW'? 97

CHAPTER 13: "WHAT IF I CAN'T?" – DEALING WITH
SELF-DOUBT 105

CHAPTER 14: "YES, I CAN – I WON'T BE INTIMIDATED" 111

CHAPTER 15: EXAMINING DIFFERENT
CHAPTER 16: EDUCATIONAL OPTIONS 117

CHAPTER 17: PREPARING FOR UNIVERSITY 123

CHAPTER 18: FIRST YEAR AT UNIVERSITY CAN BE A
MAJOR CHALLENGE 133

CHAPTER 19: IS IT A 'BOOK REPORT' OR A
'BOOK REVIEW'? 145

CHAPTER 20: ARE YOU HAVING "ESSAY BLUES" –
HOW TO MAKE THAT SPECIAL PAPER
A WINNER? 149

CHAPTER 21: IMPORTANT SKILLS FOR SUCCESS IN
SCHOOL, LIFE, AND WORK 159

CHAPTER 22: WHAT WILL YOU BE DOING
THIS SUMMER? 171

CHAPTER 23: HOLDING DOWN THAT
PART-TIME JOB 175

CHAPTER 24: BEING MENTALLY PREPARED
FOR SCHOOL 181

CHAPTER 25: DON'T BE CAUGHT UNPREPARED! 185

CHAPTER 26: IT'S TIME TO 'BUCKLE DOWN' 189

CHAPTER 27: IS IT YOUR LAST YEAR
BEFORE GRADUATION? 193

CHAPTER 28: YOU PROBABLY STUDIED TOO MUCH!! ... 197

CHAPTER 29: MATCHING YOUR CAREER TO THE
JOB MARKET 203

CHAPTER 30: CARPE DIEM: ADVICE TO THE
GRADUATING CLASS 209

CONCLUSION 215

MORE READING AVAILABLE 217

Chapter 1

BE THE VERY BEST YOU CAN BE

There is only one You, special and unique! Only You can be the Best You there is! When you strive for excellence, you do yourself proud. When you fail to try, when you just get by, you do yourself a great disservice. Strive for excellence in thought, word and deed. Think good and positive thoughts. When you speak, let your words be constructive, not destructive. Whatever you do, make it count for good, not bad. Be the very best you can be at home, in the community at large, at school, or even at work.

Where Should I Start?

You may be at a good place in your life. Be thankful for this, but know you can always improve on yourself. There are also many young people going through challenges and difficulties in their lives. You may be in this situation as well. You may be on your own and are not really sure about yourself.

You know you want to make something of your life, but there are many things claiming your attention. You wonder, "Where should I start?"

Think of the Person You Want to Become

One of the first things to do is to work on yourself. Think of the person you want to be. Tell yourself that you are special and that you deserve to be the best person you can be. You may be reckless or simply thoughtless at times in how you relate to other people. You may recognize these instances afterwards. However, once you recognize these instances, reflect on them and make an effort to change. Regardless of what others may think of you now or what you may think of yourself, there is still the opportunity to make a change and be the best person you can be.

You can decide to strive for excellence in what you do. This does not mean that you have to be perfect. You just have to try to do better. It is therefore important to distinguish between excellence and perfection.

Excellence and Perfection

In many cases, when people think of improving themselves, they think of being perfect, and this in itself discourages them from moving forward. This is because being perfect is a very difficult goal to set for oneself. As Professor Rao (November 3, 2015) contends, "Most of the time, emphasizing perfection rather than excellence acts as an obstacle to progress." The reason for this is that perfection is something that few will ever achieve, and people become discouraged knowing that they cannot be perfect.

On the other hand, people can strive for excellence. What is excellence? As Colin Powell, four-star general and former Secretary of State in the United States between 2001 and 2005, observed, "If you are going to achieve excellence in big things, you develop the habit in little matters. Excellence is not an exception, it is a prevailing attitude" (Quoted in Rao, November 3, 2015). In other words, striving for excellence involves striving to be the best that you can be. It is developing an attitude that makes you want to be better than you are. But it does not mean trying to be perfect, because as you fail to reach perfection, you may become discouraged and quit trying to be the best that you can be.

Striving for excellence is therefore an attitude that can apply to thought, word, deed, conduct, as well as at school and at work.

STRIVE FOR EXCELLENCE IN THOUGHT

First, when you strive for excellence in thought, you think of yourself as someone special, not in a conceited fashion and not as being better than everyone else. You think of yourself as having a special purpose in life, as having a special contribution to make to your community and your society. Ask yourself, "How can I be a better individual? How can I make my community a better place in which to live? How can I help my brother or my sister become a better person? How can I strive for excellence in my own life? How can I help someone strive for excellence in theirs?" Think about how you can improve your life and the lives of others.

Remember, you are what you think! Jot down your ideas. You may feel silly doing this at first, but it works. You may find after a while you have many ideas that you never really thought about before. These can be very helpful in guiding you in what you want to accomplish and how you want to improve your life.

STRIVE FOR EXCELLENCE IN WORD

Second, you can strive for excellence in word. Let your word count. Be dependable. When you say you'll do something, do it. If someone is relying on you, don't let that person down. Be known as the young person who keeps his or her word. If in the past you have been less than dependable, strive to be better than this.

Strive for excellence in what you say. One of the things we can't take back is the spoken word. As my grandmother often advised, "Don't say something bad, when you can say something good" and "think before you speak." These are two sound pieces of advice to help in striving for excellence in word. Sometimes in anger we say things that can be very hurtful to others. And if we are honest about this, this may have been exactly the effect we wanted to have. But think about it. We cannot take back our spoken words, for the people we hurt often do not forget, even after we may have apologized. We can damage relationships forever!

Therefore, strive for excellence in word. Keep your word. Don't say something bad when you can say something good, and remember, think before you speak, recognizing that the spoken word is like a 'sped arrow". It cannot be taken back.

STRIVE FOR EXCELLENCE IN DEED

Third, you can strive for excellence in deed. Unless you take action, the good ideas you have and the good words you say are of little value. When you think of yourself as having a special purpose in life, as having a special contribution to make, you have to follow through and act the role. Don't be known as a person who only talks, but doesn't act. Striving for excellence in deed includes more than talk. It includes "walking the talk".

STRIVE FOR EXCELLENCE IN CONDUCT

Fourth, strive for excellence in the way you conduct yourself. If you try to disrespect others, you disrespect yourself in the process. If others try to disrespect you, rise above it, and be the best you can be. You do not have to respond to others in the same way as they act towards you.

I once asked one of my teenage students how he got into trouble with the police and he explained that another teen ("diss'd me") disrespected him, and he was not about to take it. He resorted to blows which landed him in the police station and a suspension from school. He was furious that the other teen was not punished for what he had said.

Therefore, think of how you conduct yourself. Respect yourself at all times. Disregard those who may try to disrespect you, for they only disrespect themselves. When they expect you to respond, ignore them. This takes practice, but you may find that after a while, if you don't respond and get angry, they may find their efforts to disrespect and upset you fruitless.

If you are threatened physically, don't try to be a hero. Report the matter. Conduct yourself responsibly. Maybe by your example you may teach someone a lesson. Strive for excellence in how you conduct yourself.

STRIVE FOR EXCELLENCE AT SCHOOL

Fifth, strive for excellence at school. As a student, if you find school easy, then reach for the stars. But you may find school a challenge. If you do, don't give up. Nothing good comes easy, and the harder and more consistently that you work, the more you will appreciate your accomplishments. Instead of rushing through your homework in twenty minutes, take the extra half an hour to understand what you are doing. If you still don't understand it, ask a parent, teacher, or a friend to help you. Take the extra time to be the best you can be for yourself. You may find that taking this extra time helps you to better understand the material and this may make the difference between passing and failing. When you perform well, you are motivated to get even better. Dropout, therefore, cannot be an option for you as you strive for excellence in your schoolwork.

However, striving for success in school could become problematic if you think in terms of perfection and not excellence in what you do. Rather than striving to improve on performance, many students are preoccupied with grades. Students who become fixated on getting the perfect high grade often become obsessive in their behaviour and this could be detrimental to their wellbeing (Chichekian, April 3, 2019).

Students, in striving for excellence in school, are discouraged from trying to be perfect. Counseling and Mental Health Center (2020) at the University of Texas at Austin promotes healthy striving rather than perfectionism. Students are discouraged from setting standards that are "beyond reach and reason" which is a sign of perfectionism, and instead are encouraged to set "standards that are high but within reach", a sign of healthy striving. Other characteristics of healthy striving include "enjoying the process as well as the outcome", and when experiencing failure or disappointment trying to get over it quickly. Students are encouraged that in striving for excellence, they should not be overly anxious and fearful of failure, but should see mistakes as opportunities for learning and growth, while "reacting positively to helpful criticism" (Counseling and Mental Health Center, 2020).

STRIVE FOR EXCELLENCE AT WORK

Sixth, regardless of the work you do, be the very best worker you can be. Some employees think that the less work they do, the better their job is. Other more conscientious employees find that a job with little work can be a very boring experience. Besides, in most cases, when you work, you learn, and you improve your worth as an employee. Therefore, don't shirk your responsibility at work. Be the best worker there is. If you strive for excellence, you will develop greater self-esteem and self-confidence in all that you do. It is no secret that having a greater measure of both of these qualities is a basic requirement for success in life. You may find too that possessing these qualities may even earn you a promotion and a raise and the opportunity to move further on on your career path.

ONLY YOU CAN BE THE BEST YOU THERE IS

Remember, only You can be the best You there is, so do yourself proud and strive for excellence in thought, word, deed, and conduct, at school and at work. And don't forget to write down your ideas on how you can be a better person and help others to do the same. You may find that in writing down these ideas that you also find other ideas about improving your job prospects. Share these ideas with other young people. Form a discussion group. You may find that some of the difficulties or challenges that you may have are not unique to you: other young people may be going through the same thing. You can be a support to them, as they can be for you.

As I have discovered, wonders happen when young people find support, when they can speak honestly without having to prove anything to each other. Then life is often not so difficult after all. Believe in yourself and strive to be the best You there is!!

CHAPTER 1 - FOOD FOR THOUGHT

TOPICS AND IDEAS FOR SELF-REFLECTION AND DISCUSSION

Am I the best person I can be?

How can I be a better person?

What changes would I make to become the best person I can be?

"No matter where you are, no matter what you did, no matter where you've come from, you can always change, (and) become a better version of yourself." — Madonna

Keep in Mind: *"What we think we become. What we feel we attract. What we imagine we create."* — Unknown

CHAPTER 1: REFERENCES AND FURTHER READING

Chichekian, T. (April 3, 2019). Unrealistic striving for academic excellence has a cost. Available at *https://www.universityaffairs.ca/opinion/in-my-opinion/unrealistic-striving-for-academic-excellence-has-a-cost/*

Counseling and Mental Health Center (2020). Perfectionism versus Health Striving. The University of Texas at Austin. Retrieved at *https://cmhc.utexas.edu/perfectionism.html*

Rao, M. S. (November 3, 2015). "Strive for Excellence, Not Perfection". Training Magazine. Available at *https://trainingmag.com/%E2%80%9Cstrive-excellence-not-perfection%E2%80%9D/*

CHAPTER 2

THE PORTRAIT OF A GOOD STUDENT

Be the very best student you can be. Whether you are in high school, vocational school, college, or university, this message is for you. It does not matter what you set out to study, the more you apply yourself and strive to be the best that you can be, the more you will get out of your training and the more meaningful it will be to you. One source points to many of the characteristics of successful students, noting that these students are 'responsible and active', don't miss classes or fall behind in their studies, know why they are undertaking their particular course of study, are not afraid to ask questions, know how to ask questions, and take pride in the presentation of their final assignments (Cheung, n.d.). However, there are other characteristics that contribute to the making of a good student.

GET A GOOD FOUNDATION

However, before getting into who is a good student, you must have an idea of what level of education you would need and set about preparing for it. You must have a sound foundation on which to build. Without a sound foundation, an otherwise well-built house will fall. Therefore, make sure you are well-prepared to build your educational future.

Several other characteristics that identify a good student will be discussed below.

WHO IS A GOOD STUDENT?

Thinking of your present circumstances, you may say, "I am not a good student!" But before taking this position, ask "Who is a good student?" The most common answer to this question is a student who is scoring high in his or her class; but this is not necessarily a complete picture of a good student. While all students want to know they can score high on tests, there is more to being a good student than receiving high marks.

In fact, many students have been identified as over-pressured, both by parents who want their children to get into the best colleges and universities, and by colleges and universities themselves that select only high-achieving students. It is not that parents and teachers should not encourage their young people to achieve at high levels, but they should help their young people to maintain a balance between high achievement and being happy, moral and good people (Weissbourd, May 2011). Young people on their own should also take this as a guide and maintain a balance as well.

A good student is one who demonstrates certain qualities consistently and continuously.

SHOWS STRONG DESIRE TO LEARN

A good student shows a strong desire to learn. This student wants to learn, not necessarily to do well on tests, but because he or she has a burning desire to know more about a particular topic. Such a student may be going beyond what was taught in class, and may be focusing on investigating other subjects. This student is eager, curious and inquiring. In considering what to study, a student should choose something that arouses curiosity.

SEEKS OUT KNOWLEDGE

A good student seeks out knowledge on his or her own. This student may become fascinated with a subject and in his or her desire to find out more about it may explore all possible sources of information. These sources may be parents, friends, and teachers to begin with. As the student gets older, a variety of sources, including books, magazines, and the Internet may become preferred sources. In time, peer-reviewed articles provide more interesting and credible findings in the field.

HAS WIDE INTERESTS

A good student has wide interests. Such a student finds the world around a source of wonder, and would demonstrate a desire to explore different places and things. As the student gets older, he or she may explore different interests and may want to have different experiences.

IS THOROUGH

A good student is also thorough, wanting to find out as much as possible about a wide range of topics. This means that such a student may exhibit what may be considered an obsession with some topics or with particular ones. This can often lead to a career path that involves the subject – his or her obsession.

IS DISCIPLINED

However, a good student is also disciplined, in the sense that he or she knows when to be focused on the task at hand. Many students falter in this area, because they could become so obsessed with one topic or subject area that it consumes all of their time and interest, leaving other important areas of study unattended. This is seen in the case of some students who become so involved in certain activities, for example, sports, video games, TV, or computers that they are unable to think about anything else. Consequently, they do not accomplish the tasks that are necessary for their progress. At school, this could be evident in the shirking of responsibility for school work.

Is Persistent

A good student is persistent and realizes that in order to become knowledgeable in a particular skill, he or she must stick with it, regardless of the difficulty that he or she may encounter. Persistence pays off, and the student must be prepared to demonstrate it. This is where some students fail. When they encounter a slight difficulty, they give up, and in time, some even drop out of school, as their subjects become even more complex.

Enjoys Challenges

A good student enjoys challenges. When faced with a difficult task, a good student is at his or her best. This student is ready to discover and overcome the obstacles that threaten to prevent completion of the task. Completing a challenging task is success for the good student, regardless of how long that task may take.

Is Organized

A good student is also organized and organization is key to staying on track and on task. A student who is not organized may not know where to find his or her books and other things. This student may find it very difficult to operate at his or her best. In many instances, this student may utilize much valuable time and effort trying to find his or her possessions, and may often become frazzled, especially at critical times, when poise is paramount. This could render the student less productive and effective.

HAS A PLEASANT PERSONALITY

A good student also has a pleasant personality, finds satisfaction in tackling new work, in finding out new things, and in being challenged. A good student is eager to explore the world around. With a strong desire to learn, with a high level of motivation, and with good organizational skills and discipline, a good student is poised to rise to new levels of achievement.

USUALLY EXCELS IN CLASS

This means that with all of these qualities in place a good student usually excels in class. However, a student that gets high marks now may not necessarily be a good student. If a student is driven to study for tests, and does well on these, but does not develop the other qualities mentioned above, in time this student may start doing poorly.

REASONS FOR DOING POORLY

There are several reasons for this. One reason is that the student may continually need prodding in order to do work and will work only for the reward of good grades. Another reason is that the student who crams for exams may be able to remember enough to do a fair test, but forgets what he or she has learned or was expected to learn over the long term.

EARNESTLY ENJOYS LEARNING

The good student earnestly enjoys learning and will desire to learn for the sake of learning, and not because of grades or marks. Without a genuine desire to learn and without all those qualities that go into the portrait of a good student, a student cannot hope to excel in the long run. Such a student, on experiencing difficulty and on receiving less than stellar marks, may become so discouraged that he or she would give up. This could lead to the student eventually dropping out of an activity or school, if grades are not considered good.

BEING PART OF COMMUNITY OF LEARNERS

A good student may also find that being part of a community of learners could be a good thing (Moser, Berlie, Salinitri, McCuistion & Slaughter, 2015). Such a student may thrive from the interaction that takes place and the development of critical thinking that results from it. Further, having other students in a group could help to encourage learning as group members help each other and in the process of learning overlearn their material.

CONCLUSION – A GOOD STUDENT

A good student is one that possesses many of these characteristics. But the most important of these characteristics is having a healthy approach to learning, having a goal, undertaking the studies that are set, and keeping up with the assigned and expected work.

CHAPTER 2 - FOOD FOR THOUGHT

TOPICS AND IDEAS FOR SELF-REFLECTION AND DISCUSSION

For Self-Reflection

Am I a good student?

What does being a good student mean to you?

What are my strengths as a student?

What are my shortcomings as a student?

What changes do I have to make to become a better student?

What are some measures that a group or a class could use to improve the overall performance, academic and otherwise, of all of its members,? You may find brainstorming as a group or a class could show areas where great gains can be made.

CHAPTER 2: REFERENCES AND FURTHER READING

Cheung, T. (n.d.). How to be a successful college student. Academic Success Center Online. Rochester Institute of Technology. Available at
https://www.rit.edu/studentaffairs/asc/online/blog/2015/06/how-be-successful-college-student

Moser, L., Berlie, H., Salinitri, F., McCuistion, M. & Slaughter, R. *2015). Enhancing academic success by creating a community of learners. *American Journal of Pharmaceutical Education, 79*(5), Article 70, 1-9.

Weissbourd, R. (Nay 2011). The overpressured student. *Educational* Leadership, 68(8), 22-27

CHAPTER 3

"I AM NOT A GOOD STUDENT AND I HATE SCHOOL"

I have heard this statement expressed quite emphatically and frequently by students who eventually went on to excel in school. You may be a student who is not motivated. You may also be having difficulty in certain subjects or even all of your subjects. You may be thoroughly discouraged at the present time, and you may be thinking, "I really don't like school, and I don't like the work I have to do here."

Do You Know the Work?

Think about it. Could it be that the reason you don't like school is that you don't know the work? Had you known the work, you would probably have liked school, because you would have liked feeling good about yourself and about your accomplishment. It's not too late, though.

WHAT DON'T YOU LIKE ABOUT SCHOOL?

Let's start from your present situation. What don't you like about school? Be very honest with yourself. Write it down. You may find that one of things you don't like is the fact that the work may be difficult for you. You may find that the work is difficult because you never learned it, you never learned it well, or you forgot it.

What, then, is the answer to this problem? You may say, "I don't know the work and can't learn it. It is very hard!"

"But I Can Do It"

The preferred answer is "It is hard, but I will try. I can learn it." When you were born, you knew absolutely nothing. All that you know today comes from the fact that you learned it. So what is different here? You may be thinking, "So much time has passed, and I am really behind." Don't even think that it is too late for you to learn. It is not. People everywhere are realizing that it is not too late for them. Check out the references below, where people in their 80s and 90s and even older have gone back to school to get their high school diploma.

Why Did They Go Back to School?

Why did these old people go back to school? For most of them, they did not have the opportunity to complete their high school education when young, and had dreamt of doing so all of their lives. What stands out is that most of these older people told themselves that they were not going to be beaten by circumstances. Others, while young, may have thought school was not important, only to find out later that they were wrong. All of these people realized their dreams by going back to school, learning what they needed to, and getting their diplomas.

You Are Never Too Old to Learn

What does this say to you? It says, "You are never too old to learn." By comparison to the people mentioned in the references below, you are still young and you have your whole life ahead of you. Grab the opportunity now and learn the things that you don't know. School does not have to be a burden or some place that you hate.

STAY IN SCHOOL AND GET HELP

Stay in school and get help. Many teachers would be happy to work with a student who is struggling but who is willing and motivated to learn. Your parents may be able to help you. If not, look to friends. You may be able to help them in one way, while they help you in the areas where you are weak. University students, especially those who are training to be teachers, may also be willing to work with you to improve their teaching skills. Remember they are also students who may need to charge something for their services. There are also schools that offer upgrading and organizations that offer tutoring support. All of these are areas where you can obtain help in improving your learning.

IT COULD BE A WHOLE NEW CHALLENGE

Learning could become a whole new challenge again as you get started or continue on your educational journey. Remember, it is no use putting off your learning now, since you are at the stage of your life where your education could be the opportunity or a passport to a better job and a better life for you and your family.

Check out the people discussed earlier who went back to school in their old age, proving that you can learn at any age. All you need is the desire to learn.

CHAPTER 3 – FOOD FOR THOUGHT

TOPICS AND IDEAS FOR SELF-REFLECTION AND DISCUSSION

Why am I finding school so hard?

Do I have problems learning the work?

Do I put in the time to do my school work?

If I put in more time, will it be easier for me?

Do I need extra help learning the material?

If I do, where can I look for help?

Who can help me learn the difficult concepts that I don't understand?

Am I prepared to make a change now?

"Failure will never overtake me if my determination to succeed is strong enough." – Og Mandino

CHAPTER 3: REFERENCES AND FURTHER READING

Andrews, R. (June 18, 2014). Woman graduates from high school at 111-years-old. Available at
http://wtkr.com/2014/06/17/woman-graduates-from-high-school-at-111-years-old

Cathleen Eddison, Agassiz Senior High School graduate, may be Canada's oldest (at 89 years old). Available at
http://www.huffingtonpost.ca/2013/06/18/cathleen-eddison-agassiz-senior-high-school-graduate-oldest_n_3461675.html

Nguyen, V. (September 25, 2013). 99-year-old gets high school diploma: "I feel so much smarter." Available at *http://parade.com/168024/audrey-crabtree-high-school-diploma-oldest-person-ftr*

Powers, M. (December 21, 2013). Woman, 101, is oldest to finish Woburn High. Boston Globe. Available at
http://www.bostonglobe.com/metro/2013/12/21/centenarian-becomes-oldest-person-finish-woburn-high/BD0g88I2U4PggVciACAAlL/story.html

World Record Academy (March 9, 2013). Oldest high school graduate: Fred Butler breaks Guinness world Record. Available at
http://www.worldrecordacademy.com/society/oldest_high_school_graduate_Fred_Butler_breaks_Guinness_world_record_213287.html

CHAPTER 4

ARE YOU MISSING IN ACTION?

It takes very little for many borderline and struggling students to simply refuse to return to school. It could be a disciplinary situation where a student is suspended for a few days, or where there is an incident in the classroom or in the school yard that causes these students to conclude that school is not for them. The fact is that many of these students were contemplating leaving school long before, but were waiting for some excuse to take action. As Bob Keeshan, who played the role of Captain Kangaroo in the children's program of that name several years ago, was quoted as saying that "[c]hildren don't drop out of high school when they are 16, they do so in the first grade and wait 10 years to make it official."

Some students readily leave school when they reach high school, believing that they are old enough to take action or that they know enough to get by. Over the years, I have worked with many of these students who have been "missing in action". If you are a young person who has just stopped going to class, my plea to you is to return to class, because it may not be too late to salvage your school year.

STAY IN SCHOOL

"Stay in school" is also my plea to students who are struggling, who are feeling discouraged, and who may probably be thinking it is time for them to drop out. Maybe school has been a struggle for a long time. Many students find themselves in this predicament even without any unusual incidents at school.

Although things may appear discouraging, this is not the time to quit. It is time to double your effort, to take the challenge, and say that you would try and do your best and really mean it. After all, "the darkest watch of the night is just before the dawn."

Is This 'Book Stuff' for Me?

It may be a few months before the end of the school year or even the beginning and anxiety may be getting the better of you. You think, "Maybe I'll make it, but maybe I won't." At a difficult moment, probably when you have struggled with a problem for some time and haven't completed it, you decide that maybe this 'book stuff' is just not for you.

Don't Despair

Don't despair and don't make hasty decisions. No one was born with knowledge intact. Everyone had to learn what he or she knows. Some children are exposed to different kinds of knowledge early in life and so have a good head start. Also, some people learn easier than others, not because they are brighter or smarter, but simply because they understand more readily the method that is being used. Of course, some people may learn easier than you do but this is still no reason to give up.

Effort Pays Off

Effort makes the difference. If you know it takes you longer to learn things, and you want to learn something, then the logical thing to do is to put in the time that you need to learn it. Take the same approach with your school work.

Although there may be only a few months left for school, this is your time to put in all the effort you could muster to pull yourself through the course. Or it may be the beginning of the school year. If this is the case, then you are at an excellent place to start putting in more effort.

With only a few months left for the school year, some students may despair and give up, rationalizing their decision by saying they would leave school at this point because they cannot save the year. Their intention may be to take a job in a fast food restaurant (for this is where they would most likely be able to get a job), work for a few months until the school year starts again and then return to school. In theory, this may appear as a good plan. In reality, it often doesn't work for these students frequently become so comfortable working that they never think of returning to school until it is too late for them. By the time they think about school again, they may find themselves encumbered with too many responsibilities to spare the time.

NOT FACING REALITY

These students who may drop out now may see themselves making some money and the novelty of having money of their own may lead them to spend all or at least most of it. Since many of them live at home, they do not realize how little money they are actually making. If they had to pay rent and be wholly responsible for themselves, they could not survive on what they were earning.

DON'T FOOL YOURSELF

If you are contemplating going "missing in action," think again. You may be actually fooling yourself in considering this scenario. You would not be building a career and you won't be making lots of money, either. You may be thinking that you would go back to school in August or September and start the course from the beginning. If you had the willpower to go back to school, you may find that you are worse off academically than when you dropped out in the first place, because you would very likely have forgotten most of what you had previously learned. It means starting all over again, going through the same difficulties and possibly failing a second time!

FOLLOW THE BEST COURSE OF ACTION

Therefore, if you are struggling with a subject, your best course of action may very well be staying in school and trying to pass the subject. You may surprise yourself! Even if you didn't pass, at least you would have learned more concepts that would help you when you take the subject again.

DON'T GO MISSING IN ACTION

Leaving school now before completing high school could be a bad decision. If you are in college or university, you face a similar prospect in dropping out without completing your course. A look at the statistics shows that students who may be having difficulty at school and who drop out in the hope of returning at a later date, often do not. This could be a very costly decision as well, not only in time but also in terms of your future.

DON'T BE TOO PROUD TO ASK FOR HELP

Therefore, take the advice and do not be one of those "missing in action". Ask for help. Don't be too proud to do so. Everyone, including your parents, family members, and friends, needs help in some areas of their lives, and many of them ask for that help. If the area in which you need help is your school work, why not ask for help? You will be surprised how a little assistance can go a long way to improving your performance.

Over the years, what I have discovered is that many students, baffled by some concepts, move ahead and pass their courses, when the concepts are explained at a level or in terms they can understand. Don't be afraid to ask for help and to say when you do not understand a concept, even after that concept may have been explained to you several times. We all have different and unique ways of learning. Remember, if one way does not work, there are others that may. If one explanation does not clarify a concept for you, guess what? Another explanation could do the trick.

Chapter 4 – FOOD FOR THOUGHT

Topics and Ideas for Self-Reflection and Discussion

What factors make school so difficult for me?

What can I do to deal with these factors?

Do I need extra help dealing with these factors?

If I want to make changes now, what can I do?

Why is it so important that I stay in school?

If I leave school now, will I be able to support myself independently?

What are some challenges students may have that make school so difficult for them and what are some of the measures they can use to overcome these challenges? Group or class discussion could be helpful for some students who may be going through difficult times on their own and who would benefit from being able to speak about it anonymously.

CHAPTER 4: REFERENCES AND FURTHER READING

Adverse Childhood Experiences (July 23, 2013). Why I went from being a top student to an expelled drop out. Available at
https://acestoohigh.com/2013/07/23/why-i-went-from-being-a-top-student-to-an-expelled-dropout/

Chapter 5

SAVING HIGH SCHOOL

Grade 9 or the first year of high school does not have to be a very difficult period for students, although many students in Grade 8 tend to think so. It is the start of a new phase and transitions are sometimes difficult for many to accept. It is the beginning of high school and a new independence. On the one hand, Grade 9 can be the onset of time management problems. On the other hand, Grade 9 can be a period of easy transition for some students without any disruption in their academic performance.

Why Such a Challenge?

The question is, how is it that some students find Grade 9 such a challenge? For one thing, there is the expectation that things would be difficult and many students become anxiety-ridden even before starting school. For many, the anxiety dissipates once they get into the routine and find out that if they keep up with their work, things are really not that bad. Other students who had been struggling in the lower grades often find Grade 9 a challenge when they have to build on concepts that they did not quite understand in the earlier years. This could usually be improved with some help from family members, peers, and teachers.

Preoccupation with Fitting In

However, the difficulty for some Grade 9 students stems from their preoccupation with making a good impression. Adolescence is a time when peer influence is greatest and most students in this age group desperately want to fit in. This desire to fit in sometimes lands some students into difficult situations as they try to do what they see others doing or what they believe will impress others about who they are.

LOOKING FOR PEER APPROVAL

Some students misbehave in class, talk back to teachers, and make 'smart' remarks when the teachers' backs are turned, probably because they believe they would gain the attention of the 'tough' or 'cool' kids in their class. Other students simply don't do homework and don't hand in assignments on time, sometimes as a form of mild rebellion that identifies them as being 'tough' or as the ones that don't care. Sometimes, this is only a façade to hide their inadequacy with dealing with work they find too difficult. Again, this could be addressed with extra help.

SOMETIMES DISORGANIZED?

On the other hand, some of these students who don't complete homework, don't hand in assignments on time, and who forget materials at home, may not be rebelling, but may be simply not organized for school. For these students, organization and time management would help.

BEWARE OF TOO MUCH SOCIALIZING

Other students get caught up in a rich social life at school that does not leave much time for schoolwork. Socializing then takes place during class time when important work is being taught. Some students complain about being distracted and use this as an excuse for not performing well. A solution is to try and get away from the distraction through different seating arrangements or by simply telling others to be quiet.

Then there are the various social media sites which take up a great deal of a young person's time. The notifications that take place continually are a distraction, which has led many schools to restrict the use of these sites during class time (Ng, May 8, 2017). However, there are the distractions that take place after school and at other times, when students are trying to complete homework or other studies (Sahadeo, April 4, 2019). Taking control of time and the use of social media and other technologies is something that students must monitor responsibly.

Peer Pressure?

Some of these patterns of behavior take place in lower grades but they are more marked in high school, because of peer pressure. Besides, in high school many students get initiated into drug use. Although some school officials are vigilant and take very strong action against drug use, the problem still exists in schools, as some students are able to clandestinely obtain drugs from other students. One student in Grade 9, who did not use drugs, told me that drugs are all around, and "kids who want to use drugs know where to get it." It is possible that innocent young people are being coaxed into trying drugs and then become addicted.

However, there are others who want to fit in with the 'cool' crowd and who use drugs to be popular. The sad truth is that some of these students who get addicted are bright students with equally bright futures. The result in this case is usually a rapid decline in academic performance of formerly bright students. I know of students who have lost their lives through overdose.

Grade 9 as Path to the Future

What are some of the things Grade 9 students should consider? First, Grade 9 does not have to be a problem if you keep on top of your assignments and ask for help before a small difficulty becomes a major one. Secondly, do not be overly influenced by friends. Not working up to your potential and not completing homework are precursors to failing and having to repeat grades.

Getting Organized will Help

Thirdly, getting organized will also help. A fourth consideration is that being disrespectful to teachers and disruptive in class could earn you a suspension and eventually expulsion. Fifthly, using drugs leads to many different problems, physical, emotional, and social, not to mention the havoc it can play with your academic achievement. The recommendation is to treat Grade 9 as a path to your future, a path you want strewn with successes and overall good experiences.

It is All in Your Hands

If you believe that school is the time you work when you feel like it, and fool around when you don't, you are in for a rude awakening. When one of my students submitted an essay on the importance of education, I was really impressed with something he wrote. His Physical Education teacher, frustrated that his class was not taking their work seriously, told the class something this student said he would always remember. This is what his teacher said:

"High school is the part of your life that determines how your life is going to be. You can play around for five years and be living a very, very hard life for sixty years, or you can work your behind off for five years and be living on easy street for sixty years. But it is all in your hands."

WASTED TIME NOW, WASTED FUTURE TO COME

I think, with a few adjustments, this sums up quite graphically what every high school student should bear in mind. If you waste time now, you will pay for it later. While today students have to move well beyond high school academically to be living on easy street, the teacher's sentiment makes a lot of sense, for without a good secondary education a student would very likely not progress further on his or her academic journey.

For one thing, you may find getting into a university program impossible because you do not have the level of achievement in a required subject or you lack the preparation for pursuing a college program. For another, this poor achievement or lack of preparation could cause a change in your career choice.

Chapter 5 – Food for Thought

Topics and Ideas for Self-Reflection and Discussion

How does this apply to me?

What knowledge do I need to gain?

How do I start developing knowledge as a skill that I can sell?

What do members of a group or class think about the most valuable skill they should have if they are to compete in a global economy? This could be an excellent opportunity for these members to broaden their horizons and think about themselves in a global economy and society. Other topics that could emanate from this discussion include social and environmental responsibility.

CHAPTER 5: REFERENCES AND FURTHER READING

Amdouni, B., Paredes, M., Kribs, C. & Mubayi, A. (January 1, 2017). Why do students quit school? Implications from a dynamical modelling study. Proceedings of the Royal Society A: Mathematical, Physical and Engineering Sciences. Available at *https://royalsocietypublishing.org/doi/10.1098/rspa.2016.0204*

Ng, A. (May 8, 2017). Blocking social media won't end distractions in schools. Available at *https://www.cnet.com/news/blocking-social-media-wont-end-distractions-in-schools*

Sahadeo, M. (April 4, 2019). Social Media is 110% a distraction, but I'm not complaining. Odyssey Online. Available at *https://www.theodysseyonline.com/social-media-is-a-distraction*

Chapter 6

SKIPPING CLASSES - SKIPPING SCHOOL

Many students skip classes and many eventually drop out of school for one reason or another. In the United States, for example, according to Cyberbullying Research Center (January 3, 2017), millions of students skip school every year and the main reason for this is bullying. Some students find school boring and the material irrelevant. Some students skip classes because they may have forgotten to do homework assignments or to avoid tests. Some may even skip classes because their friends are doing the same thing and they don't want to feel left out. Others skip school, because they are doing poorly in their subjects and don't want to deal with the embarrassment or frustration.

The Cost of Truancy

The incidence of skipping school or truancy is prevalent in North America and many other countries. In the United States, parents are sometimes fined if their younger children are truant or skip school. While some school districts take action after a day of unexcused absence, others may allow up to ten half days.

While some school districts may send home warning letters or hold parent-teacher conferences, several use other arrangements including fines and short imprisonment for parents of students who continue skipping school.

For example, penalties for truancy could range from $20 which is the maximum fine for parents in Massachusetts to $1,500 in North Dakota, where parents' neglect of truancy of their children is considered a "Class B" misdemeanor (Popovich, 2014). According to Sheehy (2012), in Michigan parents of absent teens can be punished by having to pay a $500 fine and having to spend up to 90 days in jail. In Illinois, the penalty can be a fine of $1,500 and up to 30 days in jail. Forty states and the District of Columbia use fines and short term imprisonment to make parents responsible for ensuring that their children do not skip school.

TEENAGERS GOING TO JAIL FOR SKIPPING SCHOOL?

But teenagers have also been thrown in jail for skipping school. A 17-year old honor student in Houston, Texas, was jailed for 24 hours and fined $100 because she had skipped class after a warning. Although this young girl had the responsibility of working at two jobs and taking care of her siblings after their parents divorced and both left the city, the judge in the case still imposed this penalty (CBC, 2012). Between 2009 and 2011, school police in Los Angeles handed out 33,500 tickets to students who were skipping classes and who were considered truant (CBC, 2012). Other punishments for high school students who are truant in Illinois include revocation of driving privileges and being banned from taking part in school sports and/or extracurricular activities (Sheehy, 2012).

ARRESTED FOR TRUANCY

In Ontario (and other provinces) in Canada, students are also expected to stay in school until they are 18. According to the Education Act in Ontario, penalties can be duly imposed on students for truancy. In one case, "a 16-year-old student in the Kawartha Pine Ridge District School Board in Ontario was arrested for truancy after missing the bulk of her classes between February and June (2008)" (Houston, 2009). Another 16-year old student had to spend a night in jail in Barrie, Ontario, because she missed court, where she was expected to explain her frequent absences to a judge (Alphonso, March 20, 2016). In Cornwall, Ontario, a student was charged with eight counts of breaching recognizance because he missed classes several times during the year without having permission for those absences (Alphonso, March 20, 2016).

MORE LENIENT APPROACH

In more recent years, where truancy is a problem, more lenient approaches have been added in both the United States and Canada in dealing with the problem. For example, while some states send students who chronically skip classes to a truancy court rather than to juvenile court, in other states some young people are required to "attend special programs that provide training, counseling, or tutorial help. Truancy courts may also order their parents to participate in counseling or take parenting classes" (Gjelten, February 5, 2019). A school board may take a variety of measures to work out whatever the problem is that the family and student may be experiencing.

This could include tutoring, counselling, and/or referrals to community agencies, all intended to alleviate and deal with the difficulties that contribute to students skipping classes. Arrests for truancy are generally a last resort, but some parents of truant teenagers believe that the law should be more stringently enforced.

Educational Systems Serious about Truancy

What this shows is that the educational systems in both countries endorse the practice of compulsory education until the age of 18. While there are debates as to whether the policies in place are useful, what is evident is a commitment to ensure that students make use of their opportunity to go to school. This practice is brought about by concern that students who skip classes often find that they have too few credits with which to graduate and eventually drop out of school (Gjelten, February 5, 2019).

Skipping Often Leads to Dropping Out

Some students skip school frequently and eventually drop out of school, because they believe not just one class, but school as a whole, is irrelevant. Although skipping classes does not always lead to dropping out of school, many students miss valuable information when they skip classes. Some students skip classes when they feel that something being taught is not important, and that they would not miss much. Unfortunately, many students think of certain subjects or topics as unimportant, only to find out later to their dismay that they were wrong. Frequent skipping could lead to failing and eventually to not gaining the required credits to graduate. Attending classes is important to achievement.

Not Skipping is therefore Very Important

It is therefore imperative that young people recognize the importance of not skipping classes or skipping school. If you are in this situation, consider that while coping with class work could be sometimes challenging, not having the knowledge that comes from the class work could make your future life even more challenging.

BE YOUR BEST. PUT IN THE TIME

Be the best that you can be academically. Put in the extra time that you may need to study. Ask for help if you are having difficulty. Check out tutoring services that genuinely want to help you and that are not just a business interested in customers. Seek out help from older siblings, relatives, and older and retired people who may be only too happy to help a younger person. If you belong to a church, synagogue, mosque or other religious organization, you may find that there are many members who would help if you ask. Get help wherever you can, because this is the time to expand your knowledge and your horizons. And remember, when someone helps you, show your gratitude and do not take their help for granted.

Chapter 6 – Food for Thought

Topics and Ideas for Self-Reflection and Discussion

Why do I skip school?

What do I get from not going to classes?

If I have difficulties with my homework, whom can I ask for help?

Or do I find it difficult to get up in the morning for classes?

"I know, if only classes were later in the day, I could make it."

Malcolm Gladwell had a similar problem – getting up in time to go to work. Read what he did about it at *https://www.cnbc.com/2017/07/24/heres-what-malcolm-gladwell-learned-after-being-fired-from-his-first-job.html*

A group or class can speak about Malcolm Gladwell and about responsibility for getting to school and to work on time. There is also the opportunity for introducing some of Gladwell's works, e.g. *The Tipping Point* and *Blink* and for getting members to start writing, as Gladwell does.

CHAPTER 6: REFERENCES AND FURTHER READING

Alphonso, C. (March 20, 2016). For habitually absent students, a trip to the justice system is often punishment. Globe and Mail. Available at *https://www.theglobeandmail.com/news/toronto/for-habitually-absent-students-a-trip-to-the-justice-system-is-often-punishment/article29307031/*

CBC (2012). Should kids go to jail for skipping school? Available at *http://www.cbc.ca/strombo/news/should-kids-go-to-jail-for-skipping-school.html*

Gjelten, E. A. (February 5, 2019). Truancy laws: The legal consequences of skipping school. Available at *https://www.lawyers.com/legal-info/research/education-law/absenteeism-and-truancy-the-cost-of-cutting-class.html*

Houston, A. (January 6, 2009). Truancy charges only laid as last resort, board says. The Examiner. Available at *http://www.thepeterboroughexaminer.com/2009/01/06/truancy-charges-only-laid-as-last-resort-board-says*

Patchin, J. W. (January 3, 2017). Millions of students skip school each year because of bullying. Cyberbullying Research Center. Available at *https://cyberbullying.org/millions-students-skip-school-year-bullying*

Popovich, N. (June 23, 2014). Do US laws that punish parents for truancy keep their kids in school? The Guardian. Available at http://www.theguardian.com/education/2014/jun/23/-sp-school-truancy-fines-jail-parents-punishment-children

Sheehy, K. (August 13, 2012). Skipping high school can lead to fines, jail for parents. US News. Available at https://www.usnews.com/education/blogs/high-school-notes/2012/08/13/skipping-high-school-can-lead-to-fines-jail-for-parents

CHAPTER 7

HAVE YOU ALREADY DROPPED OUT OF SCHOOL?

All is not lost! If you are a young person who has dropped out of school, this does not have to be the end of your educational journey. There are ways of improving your education and preparing yourself for the world of work.

RESTART YOUR EDUCATION NOW

Whether you are in the United States, Canada or another country, you would find that there are measures that you can take to restart your education. One of the first places to start looking for information is in your local library. The reason for this is that there would very likely be pertinent information here on local programs that may provide opportunity for upgrading in your area or jurisdiction. You would also be able to access a variety of materials that could give you some ideas on how best to undertake this task of restarting your education where you live. Your state education department may also be a good starting point to find out what upgrading programs may be available. Be creative in finding out about available programs.

GETTING YOUR GED OR HIGH SCHOOL EQUIVALENCY

If you live in either the United States or Canada, you may find it practical to work towards achieving the General Education Diploma (GED) or a similar high school equivalency diploma. Some high schools also offer online courses to accomplish this goal. You could also move on to college, where you may need to have the required level of education to enter. However, some universities offer a pre-university course that prepares the mature student for entrance to these institutions. These courses allow the student to experience what it is like taking courses at this level. Many students enter college as mature students.

DISTANCE COURSES QUITE POPULAR

There are also courses you can take by distance that could help improve your education and promote your chances of employment. Educational opportunities are also offered through apprenticeship programs. You can gain entrance to some of these programs with a Grade 10 education. Other apprenticeship programs require your Grade 12 diploma, GED, or equivalency examinations. Be creative and look for opportunities that would help you realize your goals.

COMMUNITY COLLEGES

Community colleges offer shorter periods of study than universities. Many of the programs offered in these colleges provide more hands-on skills and practical experience and may take as many as three years. In many instances, you could qualify for a job with training of a year or less, but the nature of the program dictates the length of study required. There are also private colleges that offer courses, which take less than a year for you to become qualified to find a job. Some of these jobs are in semi-skilled fields. There are opportunities for study in technical areas in these colleges, which may take a little longer.

OTHER OPTIONS ALSO AVAILABLE

Be on the look-out for the many creative ideas that are constantly coming forward to develop your career. There are many mentorships and internships that become available from time to time, where individuals could train for new careers with corporations or other organizations. With changes taking place in our economy and society, new careers that did not exist are making their appearance. Think of the field of alternative energy technology where there is much innovation. Check these out and see how ready you are to obtain training that could make you ready for a new career. Be creative and remember that whatever education and training you would need to do would very likely lead to something concrete where you could realize a career boost.

IDENTIFY YOUR APTITUDE

If you are having difficulty finding where to continue your education, or what courses to take, you may want to speak to a guidance counsellor at the high school or college, where you may be planning to restart your education. One of the services that many colleges offer is career exploration where students are able to identify their aptitudes and on this basis choose careers that are compatible with their aptitudes.

BE PERSISTENT

Sometimes, you may find it a little difficult contacting the appropriate departments for information. Don't let that hold you back. Be persistent. Keep searching until you find someone who could provide you with the kind of information you are looking for. You would find many people willing to guide you in the right direction, if they know where you want to go.

Mature Students

Universities also offer great opportunities, even for people who have dropped out of school. If you are industrious and decide to develop your weak areas, you may find that you could access university study through distance studies and through programs catering to mature students. There are also many online courses offered in a variety of fields, some of which lead specifically to employment. One word of caution: do your due diligence with respect to courses offered by private organizations or individuals. Make sure you will be getting what you need to prepare for employment or what would allow you to earn some income. Do your due diligence and don't put yourself into thousands of dollars of debt with the hope that you could become an instant millionaire with the skills from the course that you will be taking.

Have The Prerequisites And Right Credentials For The Position

Having said this, be level-headed and think of how you can apply the skills that you will be getting in the course. Do you have the prerequisite skills to make the course work for you? Also, do you have the prerequisite education that employers would ask for, before they would hire you for a position that would use the skills for which you are training? For example, if employers require a college degree of the people whom they hire for a certain position and you do not have that level of education, maybe training for the skills that such a position requires may not be a good idea. Even though you may have those skills, you may not even be hired for the position, because you lack the entry level credentials.

SOME JOBS REQUIRE SKILLS NOT A DEGREE

However, there are jobs that do not require a college degree. Some people without a high school diploma have been able to make a living for themselves, but a high school diploma should be the minimum that you should aspire to attain. From there, you can build on different skills, some of which only require that you are adept at what you are doing. For some individuals who graduate from college or university, taking additional courses in specific skills areas also pays off in making them more marketable.

BE MINDFUL OF IMPROVING YOUR LEVEL OF EDUCATION

If you dropped out of school, all is not lost, although you should be mindful of improving your level of education. It is important to consider the varying positions that are available to you, based on your level of education. If you find these positions are limited, you may want to expand your opportunities by improving on your level of education. You may also consider entering new fields, maybe in the field of computer skills which is continually changing. Some individuals have been creative in finding niches or positions that do not require any particular level of education, but which focus on skills. With the rise of the Internet, with communication technologies, social media, new software and artificial intelligence, the field is enormous and ready for your exploration. But be careful as to where you choose to acquire skills. Do your due diligence. You also have to be intentional about the changes you need to make now in order to restart your education and be on a good path towards gainful employment.

Don't Procrastinate

Don't procrastinate. The time is now for you to act. When students drop out of school, this leaves them unprepared for the work force. With most countries now part of the global economy, this means that if you are not prepared, you will be left behind. Many of the unskilled jobs that were once available in North American economies have been outsourced to China, India and other South East Asian countries. The jobs that are left behind demand some skills. This makes it necessary for workers in North America and other developed countries to acquire some marketable skills in order to get the most basic of jobs today. It is because of this that you need to obtain your high school diploma or equivalent as the very basis for improving your skills.

Your Prospects As A High School Dropout

As one report points out, high school dropouts are less likely to have a job, and if they become employed, on average they earn as much as $10,000 less per year than high school graduates and have greater likelihood of being on public assistance (Rennie Center for Education Research & Policy, 2009). This report continues that high school dropouts are also less likely to get married, more likely to be single parents, less likely to be involved in civic activities, and with young male dropouts more likely to be incarcerated than high school graduates (Rennie Center for Education Research & Policy, 2009).

It's Time To Do Something

In light of the drawbacks that being a high school dropout entails and in light of the opportunities that exist for re-engaging the education system and completing your diploma, it makes perfect sense to spend the time now while you are still young to prepare yourself for a better life. Ignore the ideas expressed by some that they did not need a high school diploma to make a good life. While some people have gotten by with little education and training, we are now in an age when education and training are key to our very survival.

CHAPTER 7 – FOOD FOR THOUGHT

TOPICS AND IDEAS FOR SELF-REFLECTION AND DISCUSSION

Where can I go to re-start my education? (Schools, community colleges, universities, library, training organizations, government departments, online courses, etc.)

1)

2)

3)

4)

5)

6)

7)

8)

9)

10)

"You don't have to be great to get started, but you have to get started to be great." – Les Brown

CHAPTER 7: REFERENCES AND FURTHER READING

Ecology Ottawa. Clean energy jobs, training and education. Available at https://ecologyottawa.ca/clean-energy/green-jobs-training-education/

Hammer, K. (March 31, 2012). TDSB uses a personal touch to bring dropouts back to school. The globe and Mail. Available at https://www.theglobeandmail.com/news/national/tdsb-uses-a-personal-touch-to-bring-dropouts-back-to-school/article4219643

Lynch, M. (May 30, 2014). High school dropout rate: Causes and costs. Huffington Post. Available at https://www.huffpost.com/entry/high-school-dropout-rate_b_5421778

Office of Energy Efficiency & Renewable Energy (U. S.). Clean energy jobs and career planning. Available at https://energy.gov/eere/education/clean-energy-jobs-and-career-planning

Rennie Center for Education Research & Policy (2009). Raise the age, lower the dropout rate? Considerations for Policymakers. Available at http://www.aypf.org/documents/renniecenter_25.pdf

Texas Education Agency (TEA) (2017). Dropout Information. Available at http://tea.texas.gov/Dropout_Information.html

CHAPTER 8

TAKING THINGS FOR GRANTED?

Education is not something to be taken lightly, for the more education you gain, the more you improve yourself, and the more you equip yourself to hold positions where you can make a difference. It is fruitless to rationalize your failures, to think that it makes no sense to educate yourself, because you won't get a job. Even in a tight job market, you improve your chances of finding employment. It is true that some individuals have a hard time finding employment because of who they are; but they still have to think positive. Do not allow circumstances to limit your thinking and your achievements. With education, with determination, and without accepting limitations, you can strive to attain positions that would allow you to make a difference in your society. The challenge is, once you have attained coveted positions, whether you are prepared to change for the better, or whether you are content to sit on your laurels for having made your achievements.

Despite the obvious and even hidden drawbacks that some members of our communities experience, there is still hope to improve yourself for better opportunities. Things are changing and there is greater realization on the part of the public as to the inequalities of opportunity that many people face. This realization will lead to more open discussions and greater opportunities for all people, regardless of difference (Shockness, 2019).

EDUCATION MORE THAN BOOK LEARNING

If you are to educate yourself, not only academically, but also in terms of who you are, and what you have to accomplish, you would come to see that education covers more than book learning. It involves finding a role model, someone that motivates and encourages you, looking at the basic values that the role model holds, and the values that made your role model great. It means understanding how some people make outstanding achievements under very difficult circumstances. Even among those who did not achieve their dreams, many have made the way for others to reach their potential.

EXCELLENT ROLE MODEL

One woman, who learned the importance of education early in life, and who dreamt of achieving great heights, was Oseola McCarty. Born over a hundred years ago as an African-American, Ms. McCarty wanted more than anything else to attend college. Unfortunately, she had to drop out of school in the sixth grade in order to take care of her mother, aunt and grandmother. She worked as a washerwoman, taking in laundry and ironing in her home for most of her life, saving as much as she could from this work. At 91, her love for education led her to donate $150,000 of her life savings to the University of Southern Mississippi College to establish scholarships for poor Black young people in the United States. This was sacrificial giving, for after washing and ironing people's clothes for over 75 years and saving her money, she was able to give young people the chance to realize their dreams of a better education, something that she was not able to realize.

RECOGNITION FOR GENEROSITY

President Clinton recognized Ms. McCarty in 1995 for her outstanding contribution to her community with the Presidential Citizen's Medal for 'her extraordinary act of generosity", and on her death in 1999, referred to her as "a true American hero." Ms. McCarty was also recognized by Harvard University for her generosity with an honorary doctorate, was honored by the United Nations, received over 300 awards for her charity, and inspired Ted Turner to give away one billion dollars in charity. She was known all over the world for making such an outstanding difference although she was only a poor woman.

EDUCATION IS KEY

Today, whether you are a young person still in junior high or high school, or out of school, regardless of your ethnic or racial background, remember that education is key. Don't make the mistake of dropping out of school because you may have a job that gives you some extra cash now. Plan for the future. If you have already dropped out of school, it is not too late. There are many paths to get back on track, and to help you start preparing for a career. Without a good education, you'd find it hard to survive. Employers are demanding college or university education for jobs that before were available with a high school diploma and sometimes with less. Ms. McCarty had to do thousands of hours of backbreaking work in order to survive. She could have spent the little money that she made on herself. Instead, she was determined to save part of it, so others could take advantage of education.

TAKING THINGS FOR GRANTED?

CREATE NEW OPPORTUNITIES FOR YOURSELF

Therefore, take advantage of the opportunities around you. Even if your present circumstances are difficult, try and create new ones for yourself. Rather than pointing out all the reasons why you cannot pursue a dream or achieve a goal, think of creative ways of making things work for you. Make this your motto: "Where there is a will, there is a way." Think of those who went before you and made great achievements in spite of overwhelming odds. Then, your circumstances would not look so bad and you would not take the opportunities you have for granted.

Chapter 8 – Food for Thought

Topics and Ideas for Self-Reflection and Discussion

Education is more than book learning.

No matter what you do, no matter how many times you screw up and think to yourself "there's no point to carry on", no matter how many people tell you that you can't do it – keep going. Don't quit. Don't quit, because a month from now you will be that much closer to your goal than you are now. Yesterday you said tomorrow. Make today count. – Anonymous

CHAPTER 8: REFERENCES AND FURTHER READING

American National Biography online: Oseola McCarty. Available at http://www.anb.org/articles/20/20-91930.html

Philanthropy Roadmap. Oseola McCarty. Available at http://roadmap.rockpa.org/oseola-mcarty/

The Philanthropy Hall of Fame – Oseola McCarty. Available at http://www.philanthropyroundtable.org/almanac/hall_of_fame/oseola_mccarty

Shockness, I. (2020). Respect is Only Human: A Response to Disrespect and Implicit Bias. Vol. 6- Successful Youth Living. Vanquest Publishing Inc. Available at https://www.amazon.com/dp/1775009483

CHAPTER 9

"HOW CAN I MAKE THIS WORK?"

You may be wondering, "How will I make this work?" While there is no easy quick-fix, there is a path that could help.

END THE VICIOUS CYCLE OF UNDER-EDUCATION

In the first place, you must recognize that if you are ill prepared for the job market, you need to do something now. Things are not going to get better, since employers are looking for people with higher levels of education. If you have less than the minimum required education, you could expect to be trapped in the lowest paying jobs for the rest of your life, if you are lucky enough to find employment. This is your chance to get out of the vicious cycle of long term unemployment and under-employment and improve yourself.

SET GOALS

Secondly, once you have made the commitment to go forward, you need to set goals. Decide what you want to achieve, whether it is to get your high school graduation or move on to college. Decide how you want to achieve it. You would have to set some short-term as well as longer-term goals. This would provide you with a plan on how to achieve your goals.

FOLLOW STEPS TO REALIZE GOALS

Your third step is to look at the means of achieving your goal. On the basis of your time frame, decide on the steps you would take to achieve your goal and set a target date. If you have not completed high school, there are different alternatives open to you, as explained above.

Goal Setting – Get out Your Journal

1. Outline where you are at present: Note your highest level of education. If you have not completed your high school education, then completion or equivalency is the number one goal.
2. Decide what measure you would take. Take GED, go back to high school to complete course, or go to pre-university program or apprenticeship.
3. Check out college to see what your aptitudes are. Maybe you already know this. In this case, think about possible career choices you would need. Do your research. Talk to people in that field or job.
4. Plan what program and what training you should take. A good idea is to find someone doing the job that you would like to do and ask that person what kind of training he or she had to have in order to get the job and the specific path that person took to get that job. Follow this as a blueprint.
5. You may find brainstorming with others could also be a very rewarding opportunity that could help you with planning.

A More Detailed Look at Successful Goal Setting

However, in carrying out goal setting, you must take every measure that your goals do not remain dreams. One concept that has been introduced in the realm of goal setting is that of SMART goals.

Smart stands for the following:

S – Specific (simple, sensible, significant)

M – Measurable (meaningful, motivating)

A – Achievable (agreed, attainable)

R – Relevant (reasonable, realistic and resourced, results-based).

T – Time bound (time-based, time limited, time/cost limited, timely, time-sensitive)

(MindTools, 2020).

SPECIFIC

Basically, what this means is that when you develop goals for yourself, in order to make them work, you have to be specific about what the goals are. You can't say "I want to be educated" or "I want to go back to school". This is too general. You need to be more 'specific'. For example, you could decide that you need to go back to high school, get your high school or college diploma or your university degree, or complete an apprenticeship program or an internship certificate. Whatever your goal is, it should be as specific as you can make it, even naming it.

MEASURABLE

Your goal must be measurable so that you can track your progress and decide when the particular goal is achieved. You must also be able to measure the achievement of that goal in terms of cost and what is required along the way. For example, you would want to know how much it would cost you and what it would take to manage your deadlines. You need to be able to assess along the way how you are progressing and what needs to be improved if you are to achieve your goal.

Attainable

The goal that you are aiming to achieve must also be something that you can achieve or attain. Saying that you want to be president of a university can be a dream, but it may be something unachievable, particularly if you are presently a dropout. When you plan to go back to school, you are really planning to get your diploma, degree or certificate. This has to be something that you can accomplish by taking the requisite courses, and you should be able to take the courses. If these courses are offered, for example, through an organization that is offering to help people become literate, but does not have the power to grant credit for the courses, then you will not be able to attain your goal.

Therefore, when you are planning to attain your goal, you must ensure that the means through which you intend to do this could deliver on your goal.

Relevant

While you have set your goals and are proceeding to plan, you must also ask yourself whether that goal is relevant. In other words, is it a worthwhile endeavor, is this something that you should be undertaking now, and does this goal fit into your other needs?

Time Bound

In deciding to get your diploma, degree or certificate, you must also plan the time that you will take to achieve this. For example, in going back to high school to get your diploma, you may decide to have this done within a year or

18 months. This decision must also be made by ensuring that the institution that you are planning to attend offers the courses within this time frame.

SMART KEEPS YOU MOTIVATED

The reason for developing SMART goals is that these goals will help keep you motivated and accountable. Therefore, in your planning, even if you carry this out through brainstorming with others, you have to consider your specific needs and plan accordingly based on your specific circumstances.

Chapter 9 – Food for Thought

Topics and Ideas for Self-Reflection and Discussion

Using headings Specific, Measurable, Attainable, Relevant and Time Bound, fill in aspects of your goal under the appropriate headings.

What is the significance of the quotes below? This is an excellent way to have a discussion among group members or students to see how they interpret the following and what they see as important.

"Success is the progressive realization of a worthy goal or ideal." — Earl Nightingale

"Good thoughts are no better than good dreams, unless they be executed!" — Ralph Waldo Emerson

"Without a solid, realistic and detailed plan, the goal is nothing more than a pipe dream. And without the commitment to follow through on that plan and put forth the necessary effort, the dream is nothing more than a good intention." – Les Brown

You have to work the plan!

Chapter 9: References and Further Reading

Ackerman, C. E. (April 2020). Goalsetting for students, kids, & teens. Positive Psychology. Available at *https://positivepsychology.com/goal-setting-students-kids/*

Nowack, K. (2017). Facilitating successful behavior change: Beyond goal setting to goal flourishing. *Consulting Psychology Journal: Practice and Research, 69*(3), 153–171.

CHAPTER 10

ARE YOU SABOTAGING YOUR COMPREHENSION

Many students sabotage their comprehension by trying to take the easy way out. Given a passage to read and to answer questions, they try to avoid reading the whole passage, thinking that it is just too much reading to do. The result is that they do not understand what little they have read, and so cannot answer their questions correctly.

INEFFECTIVE METHODS

One of the strategies that some students use to do comprehension or to study other reading materials for which they have questions to answer is to look at the questions first. While this can be a helpful strategy to guide their reading, it could also be a detriment if students use it to avoid reading.

TAKING SHORTCUTS DETRIMENTAL

Some students look at the questions, and try to answer them without actually reading the passage. They look at words within the question and try to find the words within the passage. When they do, some simply copy the sentence in which the words appear, believing that this is sufficient to answer the question. Sometimes, through pure luck, they could get away with this. In most cases, though, while the words in the passage may be related to the question, they are not adequate to answer the question. Only comprehension of the passage as a whole would have allowed the students to draw conclusions or make inferences from what they read.

FORGET THE SHORTCUTS

The sad part is that at times these students spend more time trying to find the appropriate words of the questions in the passage than they would have spent simply reading the passage. Either fear of not being able to read the passage, or mere laziness, could have encouraged these students not to do the required reading.

SKIM READING NOT ADEQUATE FOR COMPREHENSION

At the college and university level, some students read the introductory paragraph, the ending paragraph, and may skim read part of an article. They then believe they know the content of the reading. In so doing, they often miss the true significance of what the author or authors were trying to say.

ONLY WAY IS TO READ IT

One point that should be made is that it doesn't matter whether a person is brilliant or not, the only way to get information from a passage is to read it. If you don't read it, you won't be able to answer questions or apply the context to understand different situations.

Maybe you do not have questions to answer on a particular reading assignment. You reason that without questions, you need not read the whole chapter. You read a couple pages and tell yourself you know the work. Maybe you do. The smart thing to do, though, is to take the time and read through the chapter. Understanding comes with having the whole picture and not just glimpses.

BE THOROUGH

Therefore, if you are a student that is answering your questions but not getting them correct, maybe you should take time out to think of the way you read the information. Are you skimming the passage or leaving out sentences from your reading material? Probably the sentence you left out is the one you needed to make full sense of the passage.

READ IN ITS ENTIRETY

Don't sabotage your reading comprehension. Do justice to the reading that is assigned. Read it in its entirety. You may need to read it more than once. Usually, comprehension of a passage is improved by reading it over once or twice. Then, and only then, you would be in a position to answer questions in your own words, and be able to apply the knowledge gained to a given situation. You would see major improvement in your comprehension!

Be the very best you can be. Really take up the challenge and put in your best effort, even if it means spending more time on this assignment.

CHAPTER 10 – FOOD FOR THOUGHT

TOPICS AND IDEAS FOR SELF-REFLECTION AND DISCUSSION

Use your journal to improve your comprehension.

1) These are the times when I experience difficulty with my comprehension.

    I am reading too quickly ____

    I am skim reading ____

    I am reading my school work ____

    I also have difficulty when I read a magazine ____

2) My favorite reading materials are

    Magazines ____

    Newspapers ____

    Comic Books ____

    Other (specify) ____

3) I have problems with vocabulary

    I will increase my vocabulary by

    More reading ____

    Looking up meaning of difficult words ____

    Creating my small dictionary of words ____

    Playing Scrabble ____

    Reading for fun ____

ARE YOU SABOTAGING YOUR COMPREHENSION

4) When I have difficulty reading, I will

   Slow down the speed of my reading ____

   Try reading aloud ____

   Try to figure out what the subject of the sentence is ____

   Try to figure out what the subject of the sentence is doing or what is being done to the subject of the sentence ____

5) I will make reading more fun by sometimes

   Reading books or materials that I like ____

   Reading with a friend ____

   Taking turns reading one paragraph and having a friend or sibling read the other paragraph ____

CHAPTER 10: REFERENCES AND FURTHER READING

Beers, K., & Probst, R. E. (2013). *Notice & Note: Strategies for Close Reading*. Portsmouth, NH: Heinemann.

Boyles, N. (December, 2012). *Closing In On Close Reading*. Educational Leadership, 36-41.

CHAPTER 11

LEARNING DISABILITY AND SLEEP DEPRIVATION

Some of the difficulties many young people are having at school involve not being able to concentrate during class, working very slowly, being listless, or probably even falling asleep in class. Some young people may be irritable and restless. These are symptoms that are often associated with one or another form of learning disability or hyperactivity. In many cases, learning disability or hyperactivity is an appropriate diagnosis.

However, because those making the diagnoses do not always have the full picture of the young person's lifestyle, they cannot identify other possible causes for the symptoms. Researchers are finding that some of these behaviors are associated with insufficient sleep.

NOT GETTING ENOUGH

Many young people are simply not getting sufficient sleep. Bedtime curfews are often extended to young people who claim that they are not sleepy, who are not old enough to know when they are tired, and who may be motivated to stay up to see that last television show. Some of these young people may even fall asleep during the show and have to be sent to their beds. Some may be excited enough to stay awake until the completion of the game. This is no indication, however, that these young people were not tired and ready to sleep an hour earlier.

Avoid Distractions

Some young people have the luxury of determining their bedtimes from night to night. With computers the distraction of choice, many of these young people can stay awake well into the night playing computer games that challenge them at every turn. Some may not be playing games and may be even finding worthwhile information on their computers. While some parents may argue that their children are learning, they often fail to realize that their young people are being deprived of sleep.

Electronic Media Likely Culprits

Some researchers explain that these media, television and computers, stimulate young people, and allow them to stay awake, thus suppressing necessary sleep. The unfortunate thing is that these young people continue to be sleep-deprived. I find in working with some children and young people that once they start getting sufficient sleep, their level of concentration increases and they are better able to retain what they are taught. Their academic performance is enhanced.

Impact Can Be Great

The impact of sleep deprivation on school could be great. Since many young people remain sleep-deprived for a long time, they are unable to concentrate on the less stimulating tasks of reading. Besides, their brains would have become used to the frequent jolts of excitement they receive from the electronic media. As one researcher points out, "inadequate sleep makes kids more moody, more impulsive, and less able to concentrate. We've known for more than 20 years that sleep deprivation makes it difficult to learn" (Experimental Psychology, March 1975). Interestingly, this finding has been confirmed over the years and even recently (Elliasson, Lettieri, & Elliasson, 2010; Wong, Rowland & Dyson, 2014; Segaren, December 19, 2018; Sleep Foundation, September 18, 2020).

SYMPTOMS SIMILAR TO THOSE OF LEARNING DISABILITIES

Research studies over the years have verified that chronic poor sleep results in daytime tiredness, difficulties with focused attention, low threshold to express negative emotion (irritability and frustration), and difficulty modulating impulses and emotions" (Seminars in Pediatric Neurology, March 1999). These are the same symptoms that contribute to children and young people being diagnosed with attention deficit hyperactivity disorder (ADHD). Some parents often question whether diagnoses for ADHD is a wrong diagnoses for their children whom they know are sleep deprived.

SLEEP DEPRIVATION AND ACADEMIC PERFORMANCE

Recent studies have confirmed earlier findings that young people are sleep deprived and that this has an impact on their academic performance (Curcio, Gerrara & de Gennaro, 2006; Segaren, December 19, 2018). According to the study by Curcio and colleagues (2006), the findings suggest that students at all levels of the educational system are deprived and experience sleepiness during the day; that quality and quantity of sleep are associated with ability to learn and academic performance; and that improvement in sleep improves cognitive and academic performance.

ADHD AND SLEEP

There are further indications that have questioned the relationship between ADHD and sleep deprivation in young people. Reporting on studies into the relationship between ADHD and sleep deprivation, Sleep Foundation (September 18, 2020) points out that one study showed that children who had ADHD experienced more sleepiness during the day than children who were not diagnosed with ADHD. It was also found that adults with ADHD also experienced sleeping problems (Sleep Foundation, September 18, 2020).

The relationship between ADHD and sleep is quite complicated. As another source explains, "Overall, there is a complex relationship between sleep and ADHD, and this relationship is still not fully understood. For example, it is not known if ADHD causes sleep disturbances, if sleep loss contributes to ADHD, or if they are both a byproduct of a shared underlying neurological condition" (Sleep Help, June 16, 2019).

SOMETIMES WRONGLY DIAGNOSED

Therefore, in class, many of these young people may appear as having a learning disability or hyperactivity and are diagnosed as such. Many parents often disagree with these diagnoses, claiming that their children are bright, enthusiastic individuals that can concentrate for long periods of time. The parents point to the fact that their children spend countless hours on their computers, playing games and carrying out other activities. Parents often cannot understand the diagnoses.

BRAIN NEEDS REST

What this reveals is that some young people are sabotaging their education by becoming addicted to the electronic media and by not resting sufficiently. Research on the human brain shows the brain needs sufficient rest in order to work at peak efficiency.

MONITOR YOUR OWN BEDTIME

While parents are encouraged to be firm about their children's bedtime, as a young person who understands the importance of your education, you are encouraged to monitor your own bedtime. Going to bed forty-five minutes or an hour earlier could make a major difference in how you feel in the morning and can greatly contribute to your performance in school. Besides, important processes take place when you sleep.

PROPOSED SOLUTIONS

Some believe that a later school start may be the answer to young people getting more sleep and therefore being able to perform better. Considering that work and school have a similar start time, and considering that school is seen as a preparation for the adult world of work, students need to face reality that they need to get more sleep and be ready to start school on time.

Chapter 11 – FOOD FOR THOUGHT

Topics and Ideas for Self-Reflection and Discussion

Why is sleep so important?

"Sleep is an investment in the energy you need to be effective tomorrow." - Tom Roth

"Discover the great ideas that lie inside you by discovering the power of sleep." - Arianna Huffington

"And if tonight my soul may find her peace
in sleep, and sink in good oblivion,
and in the morning wake like a new-opened flower
then I have been dipped again in God, and new-created." – D.H. Lawrence

These can form the basis for important discussions for a group or class as well as they can be important as self-reflection.

CHAPTER 11: REFERENCES AND FURTHER READING

Chiang, Y., Arendt, S.W., Zheng, T. & Hanisch, K.A. (2014). The effects of sleep on academic performance and job performance. *College Student Journal, 48*(1), 72-87.

Curcio, G., Ferrara, M. & De Gennaro, L. (2006). Sleep loss, learning capacity and academic performance, Pub Med- NCBI. Available at *http://www.ncbi.nlm.nih.gov/pubmed/16564189*

Elliasson, A.H., Lettieri, C.J., Elliasson, A. H. (2010). Early to bed, early to rise! Sleep habits and academic performance in college students. *Sleep and Breathing, 14*(1), 71-75.

Gaultney, J.F. (2009). The prevalence of sleep disorders in college students: Impact on academic performance. *Journal of American College Health, 59*(2), 91-97.

Taylor & Francis (2014). Secret to raising well behaved teens? Maximize their zzzzz's. Available at *http://www.sciencedaily.com/releases/2014/09/14 0926085830.htm*

Wong, M.M., Rowland, S.E., & Dyson, R.B. (2014). Sleep problems, academic performance and substance use among adolescents. *North American Journal of Psychology, 16*(3), 629-648.

Segaren, S. (December 19, 2018). The impact of sleep on academic performance. Independent News for International Students. Available at *https://www.studyinternational.com/news/the-impact-of-sleep-on-academic-performance*

Sleep Foundation (September 18, 2020). ADHD and sleep. Available at *https://www.sleepfoundation.org/mental-health/adhd-and-sleep*

Sleep Help (June 16, 2019). What is the relationship between ADHD and sleep. Available at *https://www.sleephelp.org/adhd-and-sleep*

CHAPTER 12

SO WHAT IF YOU ARE 'SLOW'?

One of the sad truths is that many young people who have been identified as 'slow' or as having 'learning difficulties' or 'learning disabilities' take this as a sentence of failure. Many parents, disillusioned by these reports, sometimes give up, believing that their children have little or no hope of making a success of their lives. Many children also come to believe that they have no future; that they are slow. This is a belief that has plagued many into adulthood and that has limited their achievements. If all through school you were led to believe that you were slow and that not much could be expected of you, it is time that you start expecting a great deal more from yourself.

SLOW PEOPLE CAN LEARN

The fact is, even if you are slow, it doesn't mean that you can't learn. It only means that it takes you a longer time to understand what is being taught, using a particular method. Unfortunately, our society thrives on standardization. Through standardization in education, all children are expected to learn the same things the same way within the same timeframe. The truth is people learn at different rates and have different facilities and capabilities as well as different interests. The fact that you are slow may be because you learn things differently from the way they are being taught. Probably a different method would work better for you. However, you may be slow in many different things. If this is the case, it may mean that it takes you more time to process information.

If You Are Slow, Put in the Time

Knowing this, you must equip yourself to deal with this challenge. If you process information more slowly, you may need twice as much time to understand something as if you were able to process information more quickly. This also means that you cannot spend as much time as your friends do playing video games or other activities, because you need some of that time to put into your studies. Don't begrudge the fact that your friends may not be studying when you are. You have to make the decision that if it is going to take you more time to understand and process information, it is in your best interest to put in the extra time now.

See It as a Challenge

The fact that you have to study more in order to understand your work should not be a discouragement. Rather, it should be a challenge. See what it will take to make you excel. Spend the extra time until you understand your work. Being slow challenges you to try harder and to be patient, for you would very likely have to do the same thing over and over until you get it.

A Great Example

An example of a man who was identified when he was young as being slow and not expected to amount to much was Joe Louis Dudley, Sr.. Born in Aurora, North Carolina, in 1937, the first of 11 children, Dudley also had a speech impediment.

Labeled

Dudley reported in an interview that as a boy in grade 1, he was labeled "retarded" (a term that is now politically incorrect), but his mother encouraged him not to let that label keep him back. Dudley explained: "When the school counselor told my mother I was retarded, she came home and told me, 'That's all right, son, I believe slow people can rule the world, if they only have patience, because when slow ones get it, they get it for good.'" Dudley also noted: "Later, when other people told my mother that her boy Joe would never amount to much, she'd whisper in my ear, 'You go ahead and fool 'em.'" Dudley therefore credits his mother with showing him that "[i]n every disadvantage, there is the seed of an advantage" (Quoted in Harrell, 2002).

DISAPPOINTED AND PUT DOWN

Although people dismissed Dudley as "retarded", he learned to read, reading things over several times in order to understand. When he was seventeen, his girlfriend told him she wanted to get married and he was happy. However, his hopes were dashed when his girlfriend pointed out: "But I want smart kids and you are retarded" (Quoted in Harrell, 2002). It was this experience, as Dudley pointed out, that motivated him to take action and to continue his education, although at the time he could barely read.

HE FOOLED THEM 'BIG TIME'

The rest is history, for Dudley became ambitious, wanting to learn all that he could, and he was not ashamed to do so. He also was not ashamed to ask for help.

When he started selling brushes door to door, there were times when he could not read some of the information he needed for the customer. He was not ashamed when the customer helped him or showed him how to read the information. With encouragement, Dudley went on to attend university. With this approach, Dudley not only started a small business, but eventually developed it into a major corporation.

PHENOMENAL SUCCESS

Today, Dudley is the President and CEO of Dudley Products Inc., which is described as "one of the world's largest manufacturers and distributors of haircare and beauty products and is a provider of basic and advanced training for cosmetologists" (Mars, 2014). Dudley Products Inc. is known globally and so is its founder, Joe Louis Dudley, Sr., who is an inspirational speaker and humanitarian (Mars, 2014).

SLOW PEOPLE CAN BE SUCCESSFUL

The point that is being made here is that Dudley's mother was right – ". . . slow people can rule the world, if they only have patience, because when slow ones get it, they get it for good." Dudley was patient, and because he had to learn things over and over, he learnt them well. He took a disadvantage and made it a challenge, and he took the challenge and changed it into an advantage. Dudley did put in the extra time studying because it took him longer to learn things. But it paid off for him, because he was persistent and never gave up.

SO TELL ME, WHAT IF YOU ARE SLOW

So I ask you, "So what if you are slow?" From Dudley's experience, slow people can still learn. It took him longer, but he was willing to put in the time and it paid off big time. If you are slow, you can take that challenge, use patience, and devote the time necessary for you to learn. This may mean spending an extra hour on work that would take another person twenty minutes. What is important is not the time spent to understand the work, but the fact that you eventually understood it. Think of the long hours you spend playing video games or engaging in some other activity.

Go grab the world by its tail, and be the very best you can be.

Chapter 12 – Food for Thought

Topics and Ideas for Self-Reflection and Discussion

'That's all right, son, I believe slow people can rule the world, if they only have patience, because when slow ones get it, they get it for good.' (Mrs. Dudley to her son, who had a learning disability).

When people told Mrs. Dudley that her son would not amount to anything, she said to Dudley, "You go ahead and fool 'em."

Dudley fooled them in the end! How did Dudley accomplish this? How could this be a good encouragement to others?

"I can't change the direction of the wind, but I can adjust my sails to always reach my destination." – Jimmy Dean

"Continuous effort – not strength or intelligence – is the key to unlocking your potential." – Winston Churchill

CHAPTER 12: REFERENCES AND FURTHER READING

Harrell, K. (2003). *The Attitude of Leadership*: Taking the Lead and Keeping It. New Jersey and Toronto: John Wiley & Sons, Inc.

Mars, E.I. (2014). Joe Louis Dudley. Black Profiles. Available at *http://www.blackentrepreneurprofile.com/profile-full/article/joe-louis-dudley*

CHAPTER 13

"WHAT IF I CAN'T?" – DEALING WITH SELF-DOUBT

Self-doubt is one of our greatest enemies, and many young people are faced with it on a daily basis. You may be asking, "What if I can't?" Some young people who may be out of school without graduating may be anxious, believing that there is no hope for them. This anxiety is real, when they find out that they cannot find a job. Others may be afraid and anxious that they would not graduate from high school. Others may have graduated from high school, but are anxious that they do not have what it takes to pursue post-secondary education. While all of these situations are different, many young people are facing similar doubt and fears.

NOT UNUSUAL

If you are overcome by self-doubt, and you are continually asking yourself, "what if I can't?" it may do you some good to realize that most people experience this feeling at some time. Adults as well as young people often question whether they are able to carry out a task. For some, the self-doubt could be all consuming. To others, it is a fleeting experience. Yet, it is something that must be overcome, if you are to succeed.

SELF-DOUBT IS COMMON

As one young man once said to me, when he looks at all the brilliant students in his class, he feels inferior, unable to live up to their standard. What is interesting is that he was one of the brighter students in the class, but his self-doubt kept him feeling inadequate and prevented him from realizing his full potential. Many of the other students were going through the same feelings.

But Tell Yourself, "There is a Way Out"

Therefore, if you are experiencing self-doubt, your first task is to tell yourself that there are other young people experiencing the same feelings, and that regardless of where you are, there is a way out. Be determined to get out of the situation that feeds your self-doubt.

Become Trained and Qualified

If you have not graduated and are not qualified for any particular employment opportunity, the issue is not that you can't, but that you haven't. This means that the solution to the problem is that of becoming qualified and trained. If you apply yourself, even if it is difficult, you can make it. If you keep expressing self-doubt, you will keep yourself stuck in a place of failure. Move out of this situation. Start thinking of yourself in the position that you want to attain. Do not allow self-doubt to rob you of this image. Plan how you will reach that position, and that will motivate you to achieving it, because you will have a dream or a goal constantly in your mind.

Some Causes of Self Doubt

Several factors are seen as contributing to self-doubt. Experiences and mistakes made in the past could undermine your self-confidence, making you prone to doubt your abilities. Other factors may include comparing yourself with others and the fear of failure. It is also possible that this could be a short term experience, with a new position or new task seeming impossible to achieve, even though you have the skills to do it.

READ AND LISTEN TO POSITIVE MATERIAL

Read or listen to material that is positive, that encourages you and tells you that you can achieve if you try. Even when things may not be going smoothly, tell yourself that you are on a journey, that you are having a small setback, but that you won't let that setback or obstacle stop you. You would go around the obstacle and keep on your journey. That is because you have an end in mind. You know where you are going. One recommendation to overcoming self-doubt calls for you to think of the positive things that you have accomplished and keep reminding yourself about these.

NO LONGER IN SCHOOL?

If you are no longer in school and need to go back, follow the instructions above in "Taking Things for Granted?" and "How Can I Make This Work?" Or you may find good counsel in a parent, a mentor, a teacher, a librarian, or other well-meaning adult.

SEE YOURSELF AS HAVING MADE IT

Besides, a good strategy to use is to write out the image of yourself as you would be when you accomplish your goal. Put it in a prominent place where you would see it often. Sticking your new image of yourself on your mirror may be the best place, as this would be a continual reminder to help you eradicate self-doubt and help you to hold a positive self-image in mind.

Chapter 13 – FOOD FOR THOUGHT

Topics and Ideas for Self-Reflection and Discussion

I will overcome self-doubt by

    Recalling the successful and positive things I have done in the past ___

    Reading positive and uplifting material ___

    Taking a break and doing something that takes my mind off negative things, like having fun with friends ___

    Thinking of a positive outcome to the thing that is causing me self doubt ___

    Seeing myself as accomplishing the very thing I have self-doubt about ___

    Taking a rest – sleep, if possible

How can a group or class help its members to overcome self-doubt and develop confidence?

CHAPTER 13: REFERENCES AND FURTHER READING

Leonard, J. (May 4, 2018). How to handle impostor syndrome. Medical News Today. Available at *https://www.medicalnewstoday.com/articles/321730*

Warrell, M. (December 9, 2017). How to beat self-doubt and stop selling yourself short. Forbes. Available at *https://www.forbes.com/sites/margiewarrell/2017/12/09/doubt-your-doubts/#1e5ca69e151a*

Chapter 14

"YES, I CAN – I WON'T BE INTIMIDATED"

If you have graduated from high school and are planning to attend university, do not let self-doubt rob you of your opportunity for success. The picture that many teens have of university and college is that it is a very intimidating experience. It could be intimidating, if as a young person, you allow it to be. On the other hand, if you are a young person who knows what you want to do, this may be the first step to dealing with self-doubt. Assure yourself that you are on the right track, confirm that you have come this far, and that you are willing to put in the effort to go the rest of the way. By thinking this way, you are beginning to push out self-doubt. You have recognized that you have accomplished something in the past. Tell yourself you can do it again.

There are a few pointers that would help you deal with self-doubt, especially when you are in school.

BE ORGANIZED

Keep a schedule of the work you have to do. Make sure that you know what your deadlines are. You would quite likely not be reminded about them, as your professor would have already given you a schedule of when your assignments are due. Remember, this is not high school. You are now in college or university and a certain level of responsibility is expected of you. Try to keep up with your readings. Don't put off work from one week to another.

If you put off work, you would soon find that you are really falling behind, and this would surely cause you to become anxious. This whole experience could be intimidating and cause you to doubt yourself. If you don't keep up with your readings, you would find when you go back to prepare for exams you would have several weeks of reading that you cannot finish before you are tested. Knowing that you have not covered all the work could undermine your confidence, and with little confidence you are more likely to perform poorly even on work that you already know.

DO NOT FALL BEHIND

If you find during the course of the semester or term that you are falling behind, address the situation immediately. Maybe you would have to double up on the amount of time you study. It will be worth the effort to address the problem quickly and not fall into a pattern of skipped readings and postponed assignments. If you have difficulty understanding a concept, check with your professor or the teaching assistant for clarification as soon as possible.

STUDIES COME FIRST

If you are going to be a success in your academic career, you have to bear in mind that your studies come first. If you take this approach, you would sometimes find there are friends who would invite you to different activities and would taunt you when you refuse to go. If you accept these invitations, you would find that you may be unable to get all your school work done. Let your friends know how you feel. If they insist on taunting you, maybe you need new friends.

Give your school work top priority. After all, it is your future that you are building. Take it seriously.

You may not be that popular after turning down a couple of invitations. However, you may also help your true friends keep on track with their own studies. You may find that you can convince your friends to spend time studying with you, and when you have all completed your work, you can all spend some leisure time together.

AVOID DISTRACTIONS

Distractions can come in many forms. It could be friends inviting you out, but you already know how to deal with this. It could be phone calls and emails. You can deal with these by having specific times when you check your phone and emails. It could be social media. Many young people are glued to their social media accounts, for fear of being left out or fear of not knowing what is going on. For some, social media present opportunities for showing off their accomplishments. Be wise and use social media responsibly. Also, be careful of what you post or what your friends post about you. These are records that could come back to haunt you, depending on what is posted. By taking these ideas into consideration, you can eliminate, or at least reduce, the many distractions that can keep you from your studies.

BE CONFIDENT IN YOUR ABILITIES

Have confidence in your abilities. Plan to work hard, keep up with your readings and assignments, and at the first sign of falling behind, double your effort to catch up. Don't be distracted from your work by friends, and if possible, encourage your friends to study with you. At the first sign of difficulty seek help. With these precautions, you will find that your university or college career would be enjoyable, though challenging at times.

Just feel confident that you can make it and you will. Be the very best you can be by dealing effectively with self-doubt.

Chapter 14 – Food for Thought

Topics and Ideas for Self-Reflection and Discussion

What is the significance of these quotes for you?

"Whatever the mind of man can conceive and believe, it can achieve." – Napoleon Hill

"If you hear a voice within you say 'you cannot paint,' then by all means paint, and that voice will be silenced." – Vincent Van Gogh

"Each time we face our fear, we gain strength, courage, and confidence in the doing." – Theodore Roosevelt

"Inaction breeds doubt and fear. Action breeds confidence and courage. If you want to conquer fear, do not sit home and think about it. Go out and get busy." – Dale Carnegie

CHAPTER 14: REFERENCES AND FURTHER READING

Chui, A. (March 23, 2020). How self doubt keeps you stuck (And how to overcome it. Lifehack. Available at *https://www.lifehack.org/567587/the-reasons-of-self-doubt-and-steps-to-deal-with-it*

Schaffhauser, D. (January 20, 2016). Research: College students more distracted than ever. Campus Technology. Available at *https://campustechnology.com/articles/2016/01/20/research-college-students-more-distracted-than-ever.aspx*

Warrell, M. (December 9, 2017). How to beat self-doubt and stop selling yourself short. Forbes. Available at *https://www.forbes.com/sites/margiewarrell/2017/12/09/doubt-your-doubts/#1e5ca69e151a*

CHAPTER 15

EXAMINING DIFFERENT EDUCATIONAL OPTIONS

In our society when we speak of education, we think primarily of academics. While being literate involves being able to read and write, it also involves being able to think clearly, follow instructions, and acquire new skills. Being educated is often associated with having attended university and having attained a degree. Sometimes, mistakenly, our society considers those who have not pursued this particular form of education or who have not attained these credentials as not being well educated.

DIFFERENT OPTIONS AVAILABLE

Consequently, many young people feel compelled to follow an academic career, not because they are interested in or have a passion for a particular area of study, but because they believe a particular course of study will identify them as being educated. How many parents start from the cradle to convince their children to follow particular careers! The reason that some parents have identified these fields is that they see certain professions as carrying prestige or the potential for high income. Very seldom do these parents think about the interests and talents that their children would develop naturally or that their children have already displayed. The result is that often young people complete courses of study only to realize that they have no interest in the particular field and do not want to continue.

Don't Feel Perplexed

Our society stresses academics as the basis for good career choices, and so many young people feel perplexed when their choice of career is not what their parents think is adequate for them. Similarly, many parents are also perplexed when their children make career choices that do not reflect the parents' choices. This is because, as a society, we put a great deal of emphasis on the linguistic and mathematical intelligences. We do not recognize, as Howard Gardner, Harvard educator, points out, that there are other equally important intelligences. We ignore the importance of spatial, kinesthetic, musical, intrapersonal and interpersonal intelligences. These are intelligences that are used in many skilled professions (Gardner, 1983). In 1999, Gardner introduced a new intelligence that is relevant for the 21st century, namely, Naturalistic intelligence, bringing the total of intelligences to eight (Gardner, 1999).

Different Intelligences (Yes, Intelligences)

Individuals who follow careers that make ample use of linguistic and mathematical intelligences (measured by IQ tests) are often seen as more intelligent than those who do not. Unfortunately, we fail to recognize the many skilled individuals or the individuals with potential for the development of other skills in our society.

Tap into Your Intelligences and Interests

As young people considering career choices, you should realize that there are many options open to you, options that could tap into your intelligences and interests. Apart from attending university and college, young people have other options. As a young person you could look into the skilled trades or into new and emerging careers.

For example, some of the fields that are attracting much attention are those of environment, computer technology, and Internet security. While many of these fields have a variety of professionals, some of these require a university or college degree, while others do not. These are just a few areas, but there are numerous new areas that need qualified personnel.

You have different choices you could make, based on your interests and talents. If you have always excelled academically, you would very likely want to continue in this same path. If you have very fine motor skills, you may choose to go into a career stream that demands these skills. You may find that you have very good spatial intelligence and may find some field of design or even town planning something that excites you. Don't limit yourself and don't sell yourself short. If you have academic abilities while having other skills, you may find it beneficial to develop these abilities and skills. There is nothing saying that you have to choose only one intelligence. In fact, the recommendation is that you strive to develop all your intelligences, working to improve on the ones in which you are weak.

PASSION AND CURIOSITY

All of this is to say, use your talents and your interests to propel you into a career that you will enjoy and in which you can excel. Also think of a field where you can make a difference. It makes good sense, therefore, that you choose something that you are interested in when deciding on a

EXAMINING DIFFERENT EDUCATIONAL OPTIONS

career. It must be something that you are passionate about and which could maintain your curiosity.

Without possessing these two qualities about your career, you could end up becoming disillusioned and bored, regardless of the level of skill and abilities that you have developed in pursuing the particular career.

Chapter 15 – Food for Thought

Topics and Ideas for Self-Reflection and Discussion

Create a journal in which you write down the various activities that you engage in under the different intelligences. Note the intelligences in which you are strong and those in which you are weak. Think of things you can do to improve in these intelligences in which you are weak.

Logical –Mathematical Intelligence (analyzing problems and mathematical operations)

Linguistic- Verbal Intelligence (strength in words and language)

Visual-Spatial (visual and spatial judgment)

Bodily- Kinesthetic Intelligence – physical movements and motor control

Musical Intelligence (musical rhythm and music)

Interpersonal Intelligence (Understanding and relating to other people)

Intrapersonal Intelligence – introspection and self-reflection)

Naturalistic Intelligence (more in tune with nature)

Chapter 15: References and Further Reading

Armstrong, T. (2010). Multiple intelligences. http://www.thomasarmstrong.com/multiple_intelligences.htm

Gardner, H. (2010). Multiple intelligences. http://www.howardgardner.com/MI/mi.html

Gardner, H. (1983). *Frames of Mind.* New York: Basic Books.

Gardner, H. (1994). Creating minds: an anatomy of creativity. *New Scientist*, 141(914).

Howard Gardner's Theory of Multiple Intelligences. Available at http://www.niu.edu/facdev/resources/guide/learning/howard_gardner_theory_multiple_intelligences.pdf

Gardner, H. (1999) *Intelligences reframed: Multiple intelligences for the 21st century.* New York: Basic Books.

Chapter 16

PREPARING FOR UNIVERSITY

Deciding what to do after high school can be difficult for some. Some high school graduates may be considering whether college, university or a trade or vocational school is right for them. For some, they may have made the decision to go to college, but may not have yet chosen their field. Other may have parents who tell them which universities they should go to or what careers they should follow. While some students may prefer this, other students may be determined to make their own choices.

If you find yourself in any of these situations, have a candid discussion with your parents who may be the ones picking up the bill for your post-secondary education. Also, do further research with respect to what you may want to follow as a career choice. Your parents may be quite supportive of your diligence in choosing a career. There are several ways that you may do this research.

A Word of Caution

A word of caution. From speaking to students and even to some parents over the years, I have discovered that sometimes young people, striving for their independence, resent (or maybe dislike) the fact that their parents make suggestions as to what they should study. At times, this suggestion may be to take a particular course and even though this may have been a natural choice for the young person, that young person may decide to choose something else.

As one young person once told me, she just wasn't going to give her parents the satisfaction to take the course of study they suggested. The bottom line was that she took another course, which she did not really want, but which opposed what her parents had suggested. This young person eventually took the course she wanted, but it was several years later. What was sad was the fact that her parents never knew how she felt when she decided not to take the course they suggested.

Recognize, as a young person, that your parents most likely wish you well, and their suggestions are therefore well-intentioned. If their suggestions run contrary to your desires, speak to them honestly about how you feel. Honest conversation could help eliminate many of the conflicts that arise over education and a lot more.

Consider Affordability of Postsecondary Education

Do you have the funds for a college or university education? What career have you been considering? Does your career require a university education? Are you thinking of a professional career that requires graduate study? These are all questions that you may want answers to before deciding on what to do? If you can secure funding, then maybe preparing to go to college or university may be your best option at the time. But these are important questions that you must consider when thinking of a career.

Choosing a Career Path

There are different opinions on the course of action one should take in planning a career.

Jeffrey J. Selingo, who served as former editor of the Chronicle of Higher Education, wrote an article in which he asked "Is a college degree the new high school diploma?"(January 13, 2017). An observation in his article was that while a degree was seen as a premium in the 1980s and 1990s, as the nature of the economy has changed, a degree has lost its premium status. Also, the earning gap associated with higher education appears to be shrinking.

The takeaway from this is that young people must do their due diligence in choosing a career path, recognizing that obtaining a college or university degree may not be the full answer. According to Bersin (July 31, 2017), "The idea of a single, long-lasting career is becoming a thing of the past". He encourages young people in thinking of careers to see themselves as surfers, being able to ride the different waves of employment that come up (Bersin, July 31, 2017).

One recommendation is for employees to not be content with having obtained a job, but to consider continually improving their skills and abilities. This could involve employees taking courses through reputable firms offered by "academic and professional experts in a wide range of technical, managerial and person-skills topics. Increasingly too, training firms offer program certificates for those completing courses, indicating new competences" (Bersin, July 31, 2017). The recommendation is that employees should continue to improve on their skills because of the fast-changing nature of technology that renders some skills obsolete within a short period of time. Being prepared for the new trends makes an employee more valuable and better able to take advantage of new opportunities.

PREPARING FOR UNIVERSITY

ATTEND UNIVERSITY RECRUITMENT MEETINGS

If you are graduating at the end of this school year, and you have decided that an academic career is for you, then plan carefully about getting into the right university.

Be sure that you attend the meetings that various universities hold. In some jurisdictions, some universities visit high schools to recruit students. In others, graduating high school students get the opportunity to visit universities. Regardless of the approach taken, it is important that a student gets a chance to obtain first-hand information about a university from the recruiter or representative, who is making the presentation and who may also be handing out university calendars.

MORE CAREER CHOICES?

By going to these meetings, you may get more information about the field you are thinking of entering. This is a time when a student may find out the distinctions between different professions in the same field, and may choose to follow one profession rather than another.

NO MEETINGS? VISIT SCHOOLS ANYWAY

Even if there are no meetings in your area, visit the prospective universities or colleges, and get as much information as you could about admission requirements. This is also your opportunity to see what life is like on campus. If you live some distance from the college or university, call or write for a school calendar, or you may be able to find a copy of the calendar in the public library close to you, or even on the Internet.

It is important to check out admission requirements quite early in your graduating year from high school.

MEETINGS MAY GUIDE YOU TO FURTHER SUBJECTS

You may then discover that you need an extra science or mathematics course to get into a certain program at one university, but the extra course may not be necessary at another institution. Considering the stiff competition to get into universities, it makes good sense that you know ahead of time that some universities may not even consider your application if you do not have the extra science or mathematics course. By going to the university meetings or by seeking out information about specific universities beforehand, you may decide that in order to have a good chance of acceptance at a university, you should take an extra course.

BEWARE OF ENTRANCE REQUIREMENTS

Apart from having all the courses that may be required for admission to the universities, you should be aware of the grade levels that are required for admission. While some universities do not consider anyone with an average mark below 85, others may consider an 80, or even a 75.

AIM HIGH

However, students cannot afford to aim for the minimum grades allowable, for the simple reason that with so many students applying, a university with a minimum grade of 75 for admission may cut off admission even before considering the students with an average of 80. It depends on the number of applicants that the universities or colleges have.

Put In Extra Effort

If at this point your grades are not high, you should not be discouraged! It is time to pull up those marks. Study each subject very carefully. Take time to review work done in class, and make sure that you understand what was taught. If you do not understand certain concepts in the subjects studied, there is help available, either from your teacher, from the school, or from private tutors. There is no disgrace in asking for help, but from my experience, many students are too embarrassed to ask. Sometimes parents or grandparents have taken the initiative to find out if their children or grandchildren need help, and urge them to take advantage of what is available.

Time for Action

If you have not yet settled down to study for the year, this is definitely the time for action. Even though you may argue that you will catch up on readings later, take immediate action. There will be new readings to do, more papers and projects to hand in, more tests to take, so as the year wears on, time will be even shorter and missed work will be even more difficult to complete.

Spend More Time Studying

If you are a 'social butterfly', maybe you should reduce your socializing this year, and spend more time studying. Your final year is very important, and would determine to a great extent which university you are admitted to, or whether you will get into a university at all. There would be many more years for being a 'social butterfly'.

BE PREPARED. TAKE ALL STEPS

Therefore, if you are in your final year of high school, and preparing to go to university, there are a few things you should do. Attend university meetings when the representatives visit your school; take whatever courses may be necessary or advantageous to get into the desired university or program; study hard; get extra help when needed; reduce socializing; increase studying at home; and address any problems immediately that are affecting your school work.

CHAPTER 16 – FOOD FOR THOUGHT

TOPICS AND IDEAS FOR SELF-REFLECTION AND DISCUSSION

Do some research on the differences between trade schools, colleges and universities.

You can check out sources in the references listed below, but do other research as well. Always use your due diligence when making any decisions about any of these schools and check them all thoroughly.

This topic will make an excellent discussion among high school students who are not sure what they want to do and who may value this exploration into postsecondary education.

Chapter 16: References and Further Reading

Bersin, J. (July 31, 2017). Catch the wave: The 21st-century career. Deloitte Review, issue 21. Available at

https://www2.deloitte.com/us/en/insights/deloitte-review/issue-21/changing-nature-of-careers-in-21st-century.html

Leadem, E. (July 8, 2018). Trade School vs. College: Which is right for you? (Infographic). Entrepreneur Magazine. Available at
https://www.entrepreneur.com/article/316320

Selingo, J. J. (January 13, 2017). Is a college degree the new high school diploma? Here's why your degree's worth is stagnant. Available at
https://www.washingtonpost.com/news/grade-point/wp/2017/01/13/is-a-college-degree-the-new-high-school-diploma-heres-why-your-degrees-worth-is-stagnant/

CHAPTER 17

FIRST YEAR AT UNIVERSITY CAN BE A MAJOR CHALLENGE

You may be going through your first year at college or university, and you are finding it quite a challenge. You are finding this very different from your earlier experience of school. For one thing, your professor may not remind you that you have to complete a certain assignment by a certain date. Therefore, it comes like a real shock when you notice your classmates handing in their papers, and you don't have a clue as to what this is all about. You ask one of the students and they remind you that it was a book review for that date. It was in your course outline. You recall that you have not yet gone through your course outline.

KEEP UP WITH YOUR READINGS

You may also find that your professor or teaching assistant expects you to participate in class. You were expected to get certain readings done, but you decide to do it on the weekend. This means that you do not have the knowledge from the readings to benefit from the discussion in class. You are rather lost and cannot participate. But you know there is a participation mark but in order to get that you must take part in the discussions. Therefore, you decide to make a contribution by adding to something that one of the other students said.

PLAN YOUR WRITING OVER TIME

Unfortunately, because you did not do the readings, you could not have known that the particular item you decided to talk about was dealt with differently in the readings. What you have done so far is to expose the fact that you did not do the readings. Other students pointed out that this was not what the readings were about, completely embarrassing you.

You also had a paper to hand it. You did not plan the writing of this paper over time, as was suggested. You decided that if you could tackle the topic overnight, you would get it over with once and for all. When you had completed it, you thought you did a good job pulling an all-nighter (stayed up all night) and got it done in time to hand in by 10 a.m. the next day. But you were thoroughly disappointed when, two days later, you realized that your paper received a failing grade. While there were very few comments on your paper, your professor had written at the bottom of your last sheet, "F - Inadequate! See me!"

FOLLOW THE RUBRIC

At the meeting, you realized that the professor had provided a rubric or a guideline that you were to follow. You wrote all you knew about the topic, but the professor expected you to give only a brief paragraph or two about your knowledge of the topic, and required you to analyze it in terms of Weber's Sociological Imagination or another theory. You are at a loss because you had skimmed the first chapter of your Sociology text, where the concept of the 'sociological imagination' was discussed.

READ YOUR COURSE OUTLINE

All of this is to say that in your first year at university, it can be a very interesting and very promising year, if you only follow the rules. The first thing to do after your first day at class and you receive your course outline is to go through it. It tells what is expected of you and how you can do well on the course. Some professors even tell you if you want to be successful in the course, consider the following rules. One of these rules could be to do the readings before class, so you can take part in the discussion. The advantage here is that you would understand the concepts that are dealt with. The truth is, if you do the readings and are ready for the discussion, even if you had some difficulty understanding what you read, you would have the opportunity to ask questions and get concepts explained.

PLAN YOUR WEEK'S WORK

One of the most important rules to follow is to look at all the readings you have to do for the week and plan how you would do them. If you have 40 or even 140 pages to do for the week, decide ahead of time when you would do them, and stick to your plan. You would very likely be expected to read more pages. Rather than complaining about how much reading you have to do, get down to reading. After all, you want to attain your diploma or degree and the only way it would happen is if your gain the knowledge and pass the courses.

Chapter 17 – FOOD FOR THOUGHT

Topics and Ideas for Self-Reflection and Discussion

1) Make a list of the things that you would have to plan for, if you intend to go away to university, college or other learning facility within the next year or so. Some factors to consider are:

Cost of tuition

Cost of living

Transportation costs – public transport or personal car

Spending Money

Allowance for entertainment

Clothing allowance

Possible income from work

Long-term financing

What to do when you are homesick while away from home

Preparation of meals – probably learn to cook certain meals

Banking arrangements

Health Needs – selecting a doctor away from home, especially if you have specific health needs

2) Think about the many things that you take for granted while at home. Make arrangements for covering these when you are away from home.

You may find this site a great assistance in planning - https://www.studential.com/checklist

These quotes may be worthy of discussion within a group or class context.

"Growing up means leaving home and becoming a self supporting adult. I think this the hardest task any human being has to face." – John Bradshaw

"Leaving home in a sense involves a kind of second birth in which we give birth to ourselves." – Robert Neelly Bellah

"Knowing how to enjoy going solo outside the home is just as important as living well inside of it." – Eric Klinenberg

Chapter 17 - References and Further Reading

Studential (2020). University Checklist 2020. Available at *https://www.studential.com/checklist*

CHAPTER 18

"YOUR WRITING SKILLS ARE POOR"

Many new college and university students are appalled when their professor writes on their papers that their writing skills are poor. While this can be easily accepted by new immigrants whose first language is not English, for the native English speaker, this comment could be devastating or even discouraging. If the professor who made such a comment is not a native English speaker, an English speaking student may conclude that this person is not knowledgeable enough about the English language to make such a comment. This would be particularly the case if the professor has an accent that identifies him or her as a recent immigrant from a non-English speaking country to this country.

"My Professor has an Accent"

Very often a native English-speaking student from North America may decide that there is nothing wrong with his or her writing skills, but that it is the teacher's language knowledge that is lacking. The question that is often considered unconsciously by the student is whether a person speaking with an accent can correct a native English speaker about his or her writing skills. Another question also considered may be whether the professor with an accent knows the language well enough to be correcting the work or even teaching the course. The fact that the professor may have an accent may not interfere in any way with the student's ability to understand what the professor is saying. This reaction may be based on implicit bias or on the stereotypes that exist in our society (Shockness, 2020).

Although the native English-speaking student may not be conscious of his or her thought process, that student may not accept the accurate evaluation of the professor, primarily because of the fact that the professor may speak with an accent and appear to be originally from a different language group. Consequently, the student may do nothing about his or her writing skills, believing that a person whose mother tongue is not English or a person with an accent cannot know the English language as well as or even better than the native English-speaking person.

DON'T TAKE IT FOR GRANTED

Native English speakers often take it for granted that English is their language and that they can write as well as speak. What is often overlooked is the little emphasis placed on the formal study of English grammar by native English speakers. Foreign students whose native language is not English usually study English by learning the rules of grammar, which serve them well even in writing.

IS WRITING A CHALLENGE?

If you are a student, English-speaking or foreign, and you are finding writing a major challenge, take the time to improve your grammar and vocabulary. Some students depend on the "Spellcheck" feature on their computers to correct their spelling errors. This is not always a good solution, especially if you are not sure of the spelling yourself.

IMPROVE YOUR GRAMMAR. EXPAND YOUR VOCABULARY

The solution to this problem is finding a good source that focuses on common grammatical and vocabulary problems. Improving your grammar and expanding your vocabulary do not have to entail spending long hours of studying. Knowing what to focus on is key. There are grammar checking programs available, but using these could cost you thousands of dollars a year for a subscription. Further, you become dependent on these and must have access to these whenever you are writing. There are also several good comprehensive books on grammar and vocabulary around, but they often do not zero in on specific problems. This would mean having to wade through a great deal of information and yet not knowing what kinds of errors come up very commonly in everyday student writing.

There is a concise work that gives you some basic but important writing pointers you need to know in order to produce good work in high school, college, and university. This book is not comprehensive and does not attempt to identify all the grammatical rules in English. However, it is adequate to correct common errors that students often make and which cause them to lose marks on their work. Business people can also produce acceptable writing in everyday communication by noting some of these common errors. The book is Some English Quick Tips – 30+ Ways for Older Teens and Young Adults to Correct Most Common Errors in Writing, Grammar and Spelling (Shockness, 2017), the fifth book in the series, Successful Youth Living (www.SuccessfulYouthLiving.com).

Chapter 18 – Food for Thought

Topics and Ideas for Self-Reflection and Discussion

In order to improve your writing, you have to read more, for you learn more about writing in the process of reading.

"The man who does not read books has no advantage over the one who cannot read them." — Mark Twain

"The beautiful thing about learning is that no one can take it away from you." —B.B. King

When you write more, you learn to write better.

"Don't let what you cannot do interfere with what you can do." — John Wooden

CHAPTER 18 - REFERENCES AND FURTHER READING

Shockness, I. (2017). Some English Quick Tips – 30+ Ways for Older Teens and Young Adults to Correct Everyday Errors in Writing, Grammar and Spelling. Volume 5: Successful Youth Living. Toronto: Vanquest Publishing Inc). Available at *https://www.amazon.com/dp/1775009475*

Shockness, I. (2020). Respect is Only Human: A Response to Disrespect and Implicit Bias. Volume 6: Successful Youth Living. Toronto: Vanquest Publishing Inc. Available at *https://www.amazon.com/dp/1775009483*

CHAPTER 19

IS IT A 'BOOK REPORT' OR A 'BOOK REVIEW'?

So you have a book report to do or is it a book review? You aren't quite sure? Then the best thing to do is ask the person who assigned it what they expect to see. These two terms are used interchangeably at times, so rather than imagine what you should be doing, find out for sure.

BOOK REPORT

Generally speaking, a book report involves a summation or synopsis of a book or article, with a minimum of personal opinion. On the other hand, a book review requires your evaluation of the book and therefore your personal opinion. A book review requires that you have knowledge of the book, its main concepts, and some knowledge of the subject matter. In my opinion, a book review is the more challenging for you have to do more than say what the book is about.

BOOK REVIEW

When you do a book review, you should have read the book and be able to identify the key concepts, ideas, or arguments that are being expressed in the book. Your first step is therefore to say what the book is about, and what the author is trying to accomplish. Having done that, you should then move on to how the author presented his or her arguments and the methods that he or she used.

Other elements to include in a book review involve identifying how the author supported his or her main arguments, and evaluating whether or not the arguments are consistent. You must also be aware of the amount of research that the author has undertaken in doing his or her work. A clue to the amount of research would be the notes, bibliography, appendices and other materials that the author used in preparing his or her work. You may also identify aids, such as graphs, tables, pictures and illustrations that make the work clearer.

Is Research Credible?

You must then decide whether the research seems credible for supporting the ideas or arguments that the author put forward, and must evaluate whether there is sufficient evidence for the conclusion that the author made. Having done this, you must decide whether the author presented the ideas and information clearly, and what particular perspective the author used.

What about Originality?

Another aspect of the book that could be discussed is its originality: whether the author was writing about something that was already written about, but on which he or she was taking a different slant, or whether the author was attempting to write on a very new topic or field.

What about Readability?

You may evaluate the book in terms of its readability: its style, level of difficulty, the author's use of appropriate words, his or her ability to hold the reader's attention, and so on. Use your knowledge of the concepts or ideas that are being dealt with to indicate what other areas you could discuss.

HOW TO SUPPORT OR REJECT ARGUMENTS

In some cases, a student may be required to use the works of other authors on the subject to support or reject the arguments in the book that is being reviewed. The purpose of this is to see where the particular author may be placed in the whole debate. A good point to make is to show what the book that is being reviewed has to add to the knowledge in this area.

Did you enjoy the book? Would you recommend it to others? Is it a book that is suitable for a general audience, for people in a particular discipline or field, or for a young or older age group?

KNOW THE REQUIREMENTS BEFORE YOU START

However, before you start to write your book report/review, find out what is required, so that you are not at a loss as to what you are supposed to be doing. It is best to get clarification on the nature of the report or review to be written. Happy writing!

This book does not pretend to give you every single grammatical rule, but gives you some of the more common rules you need to know to produce a work of reasonable quality.

Chapter 19 – Food for Thought

Topics and Ideas for Self-Reflection and Discussion

Reviewing or reporting on a book involves reading it, appreciating it, and reacting to it.

Consider:

"A book is made from a tree. It is an assemblage of flat, flexible parts (still called "leaves") imprinted with dark pigmented squiggles. One glance at it and you hear the voice of another person, perhaps someone dead for thousands of years. Across the millennia, the author is speaking, clearly and silently, inside your head, directly to you. Writing is perhaps the greatest of human inventions, binding together people, citizens of distant epochs, who never knew one another. Books break the shackles of time—proof that humans can work magic." – Carl Sagan

CHAPTER 20

ARE YOU HAVING "ESSAY BLUES" – HOW TO MAKE THAT SPECIAL PAPER A WINNER?

Are you having "essay blues?" Are you uncertain as to where to start? Are you afraid you won't get a good mark on your paper? Then take stock of what is required of you. An important part of your preparation for writing an 'A' rather than a 'C' paper is knowing the criteria on which the assignment is based.

How Will My Paper be Marked?

One of your early concerns in writing your paper should be how your paper is going to be marked. What is your instructor or professor looking for? Usually, when an instructor or professor sets out a course, he or she must establish its learning objectives. The course outline explains how these learning objectives will be accomplished and how they will be measured or evaluated.

Start with Your Course Outline

One of the objectives may be to ensure that students are able not only to learn certain concepts so that they are able to describe them, but also and more importantly that students are able to apply these concepts to everyday situations. Although many students overlook their course outlines, this is where a great deal of information about expectation is.

ARE YOU HAVING "ESSAY BLUES" –HOW TO MAKE THAT SPECIAL PAPER A WINNER?

It is important to read your course outline carefully, and understand what you are expected to achieve by the end of the course. Be sure your instructor or professor would be testing based on the criteria in the course outline.

FOLLOW THE RUBRIC CLOSELY

Now, it does not matter how good a paper you write. If you do not meet these criteria, the instructor or professor has no way of giving you an 'A'. The paper may qualify for an 'A' if the course objectives and criteria for the essay are different. However, with the existing objectives and criteria, the paper you write may not meet the requirements and so is inadequate.

ANSWER ALL QUESTIONS ASKED

Or you may cover one aspect of a topic very thoroughly, and if the paper was assigned to test your knowledge of that one aspect, you would definitely receive an 'A'. However, since your paper deals with only one aspect and not others as you were required to do, you could only be graded on the one aspect you cover. Even if you receive full mark for dealing with the one aspect of the paper, the fact that you do not cover the other aspects means that you do not earn any points for them. You do not fulfill the requirements as stipulated in the learning objectives. If you pay close attention to your course outline, the objectives, and criteria for the paper, you would not go wrong. Therefore, if you are not clear on objectives and criteria related to a course or assignment, it is your responsibility to discuss these with your instructor or professor.

ARE YOU HAVING "ESSAY BLUES" –HOW TO MAKE THAT SPECIAL PAPER A WINNER?

STRUCTURE YOUR PAPER

Understanding the criteria that would be used to mark your paper, you should then be concerned about the structure of the paper. One of the most important rules is to divide your paper into three main parts: introduction, body of the paper, and conclusion. A strong introduction, a well-structured body with arguments clearly written and supported, and a strong conclusion will bring you excellent results.

START WITH A SOLID INTRODUCTION

The introduction establishes what you are writing about, why you are writing, and how you intend to go about your task. Having chosen your topic, the next step is asking yourself, "Why am I writing this topic?" If it is an assigned topic, the answer is obvious. However, if you have to come up with a topic, you must ask yourself: "What is there about this topic that would make someone interested in reading about it?" When others read your paper, you don't want them asking, "So what?" Your paper must say something. The introduction must therefore have a thesis statement that tells what you are trying to say or prove and how you intend to go about doing so. You must make a point, and so you must have a thesis statement. A strong introduction must also have something that attracts the attention of the reader and makes the reader want to read your paper.

STRONG INTRODUCTION, STRONG THESIS STATEMENT

To make your paper a winner, you must start with a strong introduction and a strong thesis statement. Having decided on the thesis statement, you must plan the points that you intend to cover in the paper that will either prove or disprove your thesis statement or argument.

A Grabber

However, you want your reader to be interested in the topic of your paper, and so you must include something at the start of the introduction that will "grab" the reader's attention. Your first sentence or two must be the "grabber". For example, if you were writing about "child abuse," you may have some statistics about the high incidence of this problem in society or you may alert the reader to the fact in the following way: "It is a shame such a practice should go unnoticed!" Anything that will catch and hold the reader's attention, that is in good taste and that is relevant to your topic, can be used as a "grabber." Depending on the length of the paper, you may also introduce the reader (very short, say two lines) to how you got interested in the topic. You can be very creative here. Make it short, though! Remember that your introduction is also a road map to your paper, and should suggest the order in which the points of your argument would be presented.

Thorough Research

Having written a good introduction, you must proceed to get information about your topic, and to use that information either to prove or refute the thesis or the argument you present in the introduction. You need to find reputable sources for your paper. In the first place, you can do a fast Internet search to get an idea about your topic. Depending on the nature of your topic, you may find looking up books in your library may be a good idea to give you some grounding in the subject matter.

PEER-REVIEWED ARTICLES

It is also possible to find that information in articles from your university or college databases. These databases would contain primarily journals that have been verified as academic and as subject to research study. The articles in many of these journals are considered peer-reviewed, meaning that these articles have been reviewed by experts in the field and considered accurate. These are the articles that your instructor or professor would be expecting you to use in your papers. When you are given instructions as to what is expected of you in terms of research, you will generally be advised to stay away from sources like Wikipedia and opinion pieces. While in some cases you will be allowed to use a minimum of magazine articles and 'grey' literature, that is, organizational sources such as annual reports, government reports, and 'Think Tank' reports, the main focus would be on peer-reviewed sources.

BODY VERY IMPORTANT

The body of your paper is very important and should follow the format you propose in your introduction. For example, going back to the hypothetical paper on child abuse, if you decide to deal with the sub-topics, namely, the causes, the effects, and possible solutions for child abuse, you may choose to write three paragraphs, one for each sub-topic. You may find it necessary to write more than one paragraph for each sub-topic, so that while you may have three sub-topics, you may have two or more paragraphs per sub-topic. Remember also to deal with the subtopics in the same order you propose in your introduction.

Each Paragraph a Mini Essay

Plan your paragraphs. Each paragraph is like a mini essay. There is also an introduction, a body and a conclusion. Introduce the sub-topic, discuss it and then give a summation of it in the last sentence of the paragraph. You may find that if you use more than one paragraph per sub-topic that you may deal with different aspects of the sub-topic in different paragraphs.

Conclusion – The Big Finale

The conclusion should be the big finale. Just as you need a strong introduction for the overall paper, so you also need a strong conclusion for it. The conclusion should give a summary of what you discussed in the paper, and in many cases would reaffirm the thesis statement you mention in the introduction. You may also find, after going through the information you have collected, that the material refutes your thesis statement. This does not make your paper weak. It just shows that you set out to discover whether a certain relationship exists and discover that it does not. Your paper is just as valid.

A Clincher

Just as you have a "grabber" at the beginning of the paper, so you should also have a "clincher" at the end, something that says to the reader, "This is the end." Depending on the topic, it may even be fitting at the end to express some opinion or to make some recommendations. In the case of the paper on child abuse, a possible "clincher" may be an expression of your hope that people everywhere recognize that child abuse is not only humiliating and destructive to a child's self-esteem, but that it is also a serious crime.

YOUR SPECIAL PAPER – A WINNER

When setting out to write a paper, put your best foot forward. Do as much research as possible to support your thesis statement or prove your argument. At the same time, you must also provide conflicting views, which would usually surface in your research. While presenting both sides, you may find adequate information to support your view. If you find that the opposing side of the argument is stronger, you will have to report that. You cannot just ignore it. This weakens your paper.

If you have not had much success in the past in writing a good paper, don't accept that you could never improve. If you can write a 'C' paper, you can just as easily write a paper that receives an 'A'. Some students think of themselves as 'C' students, because they receive 'Cs' on most of their papers. This does not have to be the case. Think about it. To get a 'C', you have to work quite hard to get probably about 65 to 70 points. To get an 'A' you have to work to get an extra 15 or 20 points. If you are able to put in the effort to get 70 points, why should it be such a struggle to get another 10 or 20 points?

THE SECRET

The secret is in following the guidelines given by your professor or instructor, including the sources that were recommended, and sources that were used in your course, if this is allowed. Do adequate research and write accurately. Proofread your work and if you are unsure of the spelling of a word, don't guess. Take the time and check it out in a dictionary.

CHAPTER 20 – FOOD FOR THOUGHT

Topics and Ideas for Self-Reflection and Discussion

Structure a paper on a subject of your choice

Topic – What is the topic you will be discussing?

Introduction:

    Grabber – Say something extraordinary or exciting about your topic.

    Rest of introduction – What are you going to say about your

    topic?

    Write out your thesis statement here. It must have 3 points:

        a)

        b)

        c)

Body of Paper

    First, discuss the first point of your thesis statement

    Second, discuss the second point of your thesis statement

    Third, discuss the third point of your thesis statement

Conclusion:

Give summation of what you said in the three points in your paper. Discuss whether your thesis statement was proven or refuted. Maybe give your opinion on the subject or make a recommendation.

Clincher – A statement that reflects on the topic and shows that it is the end of the paper.

CHAPTER 21

IMPORTANT SKILLS FOR SUCCESS IN SCHOOL, LIFE, AND WORK

If young people are to overcome school failure and be prepared for a success in school, life, and work in the 21st century, there are certain skills that they need to have. Speaking broadly, we will recognize that these are literacy skills, numeracy skills, learning skills, problem-solving skills, life skills, and job skills. Speaking more narrowly, we will further point out that these skills can be further broken down into other skills or sub-skills. These will all be dealt with below.

LITERACY SKILLS

Literacy skills are often thought of as referring to the usual skills associated with young children being able to read, spell and use language. But literacy skills cover much more than these. Having literacy skills in today's society involves being able to find information in this highly digital environment and being able to distinguish between what is credible and what is not. Literacy skills also apply to how an individual uses the information the various media provide and this is closely linked with the individual's ability to sift out pertinent information from all the 'noise'.

Literacy also pertains to the various technologies that are available today. Ask yourself, "Do I know how to use the various technologies that are around?" "Do I know the etiquette that is appropriate for using different social networking sites?" "Do I know how to target social networking sites and use these as a means of reaching potential customers?" "Do I know how to use the various software packages and programs that are available to get work done?" "Can I get a job working for an organization that is highly digital?" Many organizations are more willing to hire individuals who are able to help them promote their visibility and increase their productivity online and in different markets.

Many organizations have older employees in managerial and leadership positions who find it a challenge working digitally. Many of these older employees have not acquired the new skills; some have, but may not feel comfortable working with these skills. Having younger employees with these digital skills is highly valued in many of these organizations. Younger workers who have a plethora of these skills will find themselves in high demand as technology becomes even more advanced. A leading field today is that of Artificial Intelligence or AI and it is fast becoming a very lucrative field requiring highly skilled employees. Having the skills to work in this field puts younger workers at a high premium.

NUMERACY SKILLS

Numeracy skills are often thought of as referring to the ability to add, subtract, multiply and divide, and having the ability to understand these operations. Being able to understand equations is also an important aspect of numeracy.

Knowing how to manipulate these operations to solve everyday problems is also significant. But numeracy covers even more than this. It involves having good number sense, having good operations sense, understanding computation, measurement, and geometry, and more than that, understanding probability and statistics. Statistics is very important in analysis and so plays an important part in AI. Numeracy also involves the ability to reason and apply numerical concepts to this reasoning.

Consequently, literacy and numeracy, while referring to basic skills that young children need to have in grade school, are also skills that adults should have if they are to function well in the 21st century society and if they are going to be able to hold in-demand jobs.

Learning Skills

Learning skills are also important and pertain to how people learn. Do you learn by accepting what you read, what you are told, and/or what you know others believe? Do you allow others in positions of authority to tell you what you should think because you believe they know better than you do? Or are you a critical thinker who reads widely, listens intently to a variety of different views and then uses critical thinking in order to understand things better.

Learning skills therefore cover the manner in which individuals learn and these are said to include critical thinking, creative thinking, communicating, and collaborating. These skills may also be covered under the rubric of problem solving skills.

Problem Solving Skills

Critical thinking skills require you to be able to analyze an issue, find out all there is to know about it, evaluate it and use the knowledge gained for problem solving. One of the learning skills that employers are looking for is that of critical thinking. Employees are called upon to solve problems and this could only take place after they have analyzed, evaluated and made decisions based on all the information they have gathered regarding a particular issue or incident.

Creative thinking is another important learning skill that helps in solving problems and are skills that employers are looking for. Creative thinking is where a potential employee is able to think outside the box. This kind of thinking also supports innovation and is instrumental when people are able to collaborate with others, bring new ideas to the table and communicate well in a team setting. These are all skills that are highly valued in everyday living and in a work environment. Creativity and imagination are therefore high on the characteristics employers look for in prospective employees.

LIFE SKILLS

You will find that life skills are very important for you as well as for your employer. Questions an employer may want to find out are how productive you are, whether you are good at time management, whether you have leadership potential, whether you are able to adapt to changing circumstances, and whether you can work under pressure. Employers may also want to know whether you are an innovative individual, entrepreneurial in outlook and can get along with others. Collaboration, communication and teamwork are therefore important life skills that are necessary for getting along with others, but are also skills employers want in their employees (Soffel, March 10, 2016).

Interpersonal skills are also included under life skills. Equally important are whether you are able to use empathy and relate to others in the organization, and whether you are able to get along with people who are diverse in terms of age, gender, race, sexual orientation and the like. Are you able to consider different points of view, particularly as our work force is now made up of at least three generations with different perceptions of how work is to be done? Are you respectful to your fellow employees and to their ideas? All of these considerations would go into supporting a work environment that is harmonious and productive. (Corporate Finance Institute, 2020).

Basically, the skills young people need to develop are those related to emotional intelligence, where individuals are not only aware of themselves, but are aware of, and care for, others, have the ability to show empathy towards other people, can manifest patience when dealing with others, and naturally show respect to others (Shockness, 2017).

JOB SKILLS

However, as young people move out of the teenage years, as they approach adulthood and take on the responsibilities that go with their new status, concerns about making a living loom quite high. For some young people, the concern is getting a job right away to pay for basic necessities. This often involves turning part time employment into full time activity. For other young people, this liminal period is characterized by continued part time employment and efforts to embark more seriously on career planning.

Except these young people have specific professions or careers that they had been planning for a while, this period very likely may involve thinking about the skills that are in demand in today's marketplace and in this climate of pandemic. It is good to keep in mind that even when the pandemic is over, there would be further transformations taking place in employment opportunities. One way of thinking about skills is to look at the types of job skills that are needed, including literacy skills, numeracy skills, learning skills, problem solving skills, and life skills, and all the other sub-skills that are related to these higher level skills.

SKILLS EMPLOYERS WANT IN EMPLOYEES

Most people put high store on technical skills as what employers are looking for. While this is mostly true, employers are looking for much more than technical skills. As one source points out, "According to a recent LinkedIn survey of 291 hiring managers, interpersonal skills are both more important and also harder to find" (Corporate Finance Institute, 2020). It is therefore important as a prospective employee to recognize that while job skills are important, employers want employees who possess complex problem-solving skills, critical thinking skills, negotiation skills, creativity, and emotional intelligence. Employers are also looking for employees who are able to manage people, coordinate with others, make good judgment and carry out sound decision-making. Besides, the employees that are in demand are those who are service-oriented and who can switch comfortably between thinking about different issues (Hansen, March 27, 2018). Young people seeking employment should ensure that they have these skills and should try to develop the skills they know they will need.

EMPLOYEE PREPARATION FOR EMPLOYMENT

Employees who want to be in demand must therefore acquire as many of these skills as possible, and must consider that with this changing economic climate having as many of these skills as possible holds great prospects for them. Having job skills that are transferable is also another strategy for employees. Employers and business leaders recognize that there are many changes, many of them technological, which can transform their businesses overnight. This means employers want to be prepared for such changes. Employees with transferable skills including computing skills are therefore at a premium as they can jump in quickly into a new role if they have the skills to do the work. Other than that, employers would have to retrain and reskill old employees to try to do the new jobs, which would necessarily take time. Or these employers would have to look for new employees with the skills they need, which could also take time, particularly if there are shortages of workers with these skills.

EXAMPLE OF AN AREA IN DEMAND

Computer technology has had a leveling effect, making it possible for some young people with less academic education to acquire higher level positions. Computer technology has also made it possible for many higher level jobs to become more specialized. Literacy, numeracy and computer skills are necessary and students everywhere must focus on acquiring these skills if they want to be gainfully employed in the economy, especially in the future. So important have computer skills become that a study done on New York City encouraged authorities to focus on computer technology education from elementary years (Dvorkin, Amandolare, Chambers & Shaviro, 2020). This same study also recommends training for adults in this field in order to enable the city to fill its demand for labour in the coming years (Dvorkin et al., 2020).

Artificial Intelligence (AI)

Artificial Intelligence (AI), which was once the subject of great science fiction works, has not only become reality, but is increasingly being adopted in many fields. Very basically, AI is any artificial system that can act rationally, think or act as a human being, and can carry out activities without oversight by humans (Viski, Jones, Rand, Boyce, & Siegel, 2020). It is seen in the use of robots and in various forms of automation in a variety of applications (West, 2018).

Some job opportunities for AI are found in healthcare, engineering and construction, business and marketing, national security and in transportation and city planning (Vicki et al., 2020). These are all fields that continue to grow and where computer science knowledge can prove to be an important aspect of preparing for employment in any of these fields. AI knowledge may prove to give a prospective employee a competitive advantage over other competitors for the same job. Other fields where AI is also used are varied commercial activities, government, politics, and global international relations. With AI being such an important and growing technology, students in different fields can look at how AI is being practiced in their field or profession and see if there are opportunities open to them there.

Seizing an Opportunity

Here's something I read about only a short while ago. One young man who dropped out of high school at 19 was able to get into college in his late 20s, but eventually dropped out of college shortly afterwards. At 29, desperate to find a career, he took up computer coding. After some short term employment, he was able to go on to become a highly paid consultant in the field without having a degree in computer science. While this was a lucky break for this young man, it just goes to show how determination (and possibly desperation) led to an opportunity for this young man in technology and a brighter future. This was one person's experience and should not be seen as encouraging lack of planning. But it does show the importance of checking out possibilities and taking advantage of opportunities. More than that, it says, "Believe in yourself. You can do it."

A Sampling of Positions and Companies in AI

Speaking about possible careers in AI, one source highlights five top careers in AI, namely, Machine Learning Engineer, Data Scientist, Business Intelligence Developer, Research Scientist, and Big Data Engineer (Zola, September 5, 2018). Several companies have already been hiring employees with AI expertise. Some of these include Amazon, Microsoft, IBM, Facebook, Intel, Samsung, Lenovo, Uber and Wells Fargo (Zola, September 5, 2018). For other companies, seek out Zola's article in our references.

Successful Youth Living advocates being prepared for the future and taking whatever measures are necessary to make that preparation possible. It encourages young people everywhere to pay attention to the development of appropriate literacy skills, numeracy skills, learning skills, problem-solving skills, and life skills, while embracing useful job skills. The future belongs to those who possess job skills, and who also possess interpersonal and the softer skills that equip them to fit in and respect their fellow humans at work and in the community at large.

CHAPTER 21 – FOOD FOR THOUGHT

TOPICS AND IDEAS FOR SELF-REFLECTION AND DISCUSSION

Make a list with the following:

1. Take an inventory of your present job skills (Recall the jobs you may have had and the skills you have developed through training and education).

2. Take an inventory of the job skills you would like to have and positions you would like to hold.

3. Take an inventory of the various skills you possess
    a. Literacy Skills
    b. Numeracy Skills
    c. Learning Skills
    d. Problem Solving Skills
    e. Life Skills

4. Take an inventory of all the various skills that you would like to develop.

CHAPTER 21: REFERENCES AND FURTHER READING

Corporate Finance Institute (2020). Interpersonal Skills: Why interpersonal skills matter and how to improve them. Available at *https://corporatefinanceinstitute.com/resources/careers/soft-skills/interpersonal-skills/*

Dvorkin, E., Amandolare, S., Chambers, J. & Shaviro, C. (2020). Plugging in: Building NYC's tech education & training ecosystem. Center for an Urban Future. Available at nycfuture.org. February *https://www.jstor.org/stable/pdf/resrep21895.pdf?ab_segments=0%252Fbasic_SYC-5187_SYC-5188%252F5187&refreqid=excelsior%3A299bd9bf36d54f1ac1ae3affe4870476*

Hansen, M. E. (March 27, 2018). Higher education needs dusting off for the 21st century. World Economic Forum. Available at *https://www.weforum.org/agenda/2018/03,make-higher-education-skills-relevant-for-students*

Kavanagh, C. (2019). *Artificial Intelligence: An Opportunity to Craft Smarter Responses*. Carnegie Endowment for International Peace.

Soffel, J. (March 10, 2016). What are the 21st-century skills every student needs? World Economic Forum. Available at *https://www.weforum.org/agenda/2016/03/21st-century-skills-future-jobs-students*.

Stauffler, B. (March 19, 2020). What are 21st Century Skills? Available at *https://www.aeseducation.com/blog/what-are-21st-century-skills*

Viski, A., Jones, S., Rand, L., Boyce, T. & Siegel, J. (2020). *Artificial intelligence and strategic trade controls.* Center for International & Security Studies.

West, D. M. (2018). *The Future of Work: Robots, AI, and Automation.* U.S.: Brookings Institution Press.

Zola, A. (September 5, 2018). 5 Careers in Artificial Intelligence. Available at https://www.springboard.com/blog/5-careers-in-artificial-intelligence

Shockness, I. (2017). Developing Emotional Intelligence:30 Ways for Older Teens and Young Adults to Develop Their Caring Capacities. Vanquest Publishing Inc.

CHAPTER 22

WHAT WILL YOU BE DOING THIS SUMMER?

As usual, many young people are anxiously looking for summer employment. Other young people have already secured summer jobs or are returning to the jobs they had last summer. For some, these summer jobs will make the difference between their going back to school in the Fall, and having to take some time away from school to build up more financial resources. For others, having a job is a means of gaining important skills.

SUMMER JOB MORE THAN MAKING MONEY

Many young people take any job during the summer, since making money may be their sole concern. Summer jobs provide the opportunity to earn money but for others it is a time of finding out what they want to do as a career. Many young people change career choices, based on their summer experience. Probably a field that has never appealed to a student starts looking attractive after the student has worked in a particular job for the summer.

JOBS COULD BE GOOD TRAINING GROUND

At the same time, some jobs are very different from what the young person wants to do. Even so, these jobs could be very good training ground. Young people learn about responsibility, about hard work, about being on time, and about having people depend upon them. Besides, young people may learn many life skills that pay off later on.

On the other hand, there are some young people who may live at home, whose parents may be paying their school fees, or who may be receiving student loans. While getting a summer job is important, not getting one may not jeopardize their going back to school.

PUT YOUR BEST EFFORT FORWARD REGARDLESS OF THE JOB

Regardless of the situation, if you are a young person who is going to be working this summer, put your best effort forward. You may not be doing your favorite work, and in short, it may be backbreaking work with long hours. Even so, treat the job as the best job you could ever have. Be punctual, don't waste time and don't be sloppy. Dress appropriately for the job. Look for opportunities to be more efficient, and get along with your work mates. Work can be so much more fun when it is done in a friendly rather than a hostile or unpleasant atmosphere!!

PREPARE YOURSELF FOR CHANGING CAREERS

Also, it makes good sense to learn as much as you can about a job, and to develop as many skills as possible while you are young. This is necessary, for according to human resource specialists, the average person getting into the work force today would have to change careers several times. This means that the average young person must have an arsenal of skills that will equip him or her to adapt to the world of work.

VOLUNTEERING IS AN OPTION

If you are a young person who did not get a job or who is looking for experience and training rather than money, then volunteering in your chosen field or in a related field may be your answer. It is also possible that you are a young person who is not sure that you made the right career choice, or maybe you have not yet decided on what you want to do. Use the summer wisely. Decide what field you want to explore or learn more about.

Look for organizations that are in the particular field. Speak to personnel in these organizations about being a volunteer. Many organizations will welcome a young person who wants to find out more about a career or a field. I have known of several cases where volunteering has led to full time careers or to employment consideration after the young person has acquired his or her training.

USE SUMMER WISELY

Therefore, if you are a young person looking for a job, for experience and training, or for greater knowledge about a particular field, use this summer wisely. Go about a job search seriously, know why you are looking for a summer job and what is most important about getting one. If you are looking for experience and training, see where you would gain most, either in a job setting or in a volunteer placement. If you are trying to make up your mind about a career, you may find a particular volunteer position is your answer, or you may have to look at different ones. Whichever decision you make, remember to be considerate, and if you are looking to gain something, you must be willing to give something in return. People are only too willing to help those who are willing to help others.

CHAPTER 23

HOLDING DOWN THAT PART-TIME JOB

Maybe you did not get a summer job, and you need money for the school year. You may decide to get a part-time job while at school. Or maybe you just want to have more money to spend while at school. One of the greatest feelings for a young person is getting your first paycheck. Getting a part-time job marks the beginning of the path to independence, for now you can buy some of the things you want, without having to ask and be told 'No". For some of you, having a part-time job means being able to help out and this could be a very empowering experience, since you are making an important contribution by assuming responsibility.

It's My Money

However, many young people take the position, "It is my money, and I can buy what I want," and they often spend everything that they make. As one parent once told me, "It's really a waste, because she (her daughter) doesn't really need half the things she buys." Yet, this young girl put in as many hours as she was able to do at work. Most young people, especially those starting to work for the first time, find the excitement of working and of having their own money to spend and sometimes to save. Many wish this thrill would last indefinitely. If you are a young person in this situation, you may be able to identify with this feeling.

Does Work Compete with School?

However, despite the thrill and the feeling of independence and empowerment that go with the paycheck, there are some important factors to consider. One of the most important is whether work is competing with school. Most young people would say it doesn't, and for some, this is true. For others, the competition is obvious. This is particularly true when a young person has to fit in hours of work after school, and sometimes even between classes.

Be Honest with Yourself

As a young person, you have to be honest with yourself. Do you find that at times you have to make a choice between doing homework and working at your part-time job? Do you find that you are continually not completing your homework? Are there times when you have to sacrifice the amount of time you study for an exam? Are there times when you wish you had the evening off before an important test, but instead you had to work late? Do you have difficulty keeping your eyes open in class? Have your grades dropped since you took on your part-time job? Does your supervisor not care that you are a student, and that you are not able to put in thirty hours for the week? If you answer these questions truthfully to yourself, and you realize that your schoolwork has taken second place to your part-time job, then you have to seriously reconsider what you are doing. Your priorities may be out of balance.

Stop Working May Be the Answer

Many parents would say "Stop working!" and sometimes this is the best answer. But there are times when, as a young person, you need to learn to be responsible and develop a sense of independence. You may also need to learn the value of things and you may need to realize that, in many instances, your parents make sacrifices to provide for you. "Stop working" is the best answer, though, if you are neglecting your schoolwork, and not showing as much interest in school as you should. Getting too involved in the work force while going to school could negatively impact your school work, and your prospect of staying in school.

BENEFITS AS WELL AS DISADVANTAGES

Working while going to school is seen as having some advantages for it can provide development of independence and the acquisition of many useful skills. Students get a firsthand experience of what it means to be in the labor force and the responsibilities that go with it (Staff & Schulenberg, 2010). But studies show that the dropout rate increases when students spend more than 15 hours a week doing paid work. Other observations among working students show a decrease in academic performance, less involvement with schooling, and an increase in misconduct. Young men are said to be more likely to drop out of school after 20 hours of work per week than are young women (Staff & Schulenberg, 2010).

MORE THAN 20 HOURS CAN BE A BUST

According to Staff, Schulenberg, and Bachman (2010), "Teenagers working more than 20 hours per week perform worse in school than youth who work less." There are two main explanations for this.

Students who work a lot of hours tend to put more time into their work than in completing homework, spend less time preparing for exams, and participate less in extracurricular activities. They also do not have the time to get help from their parents and teachers. High intensity part-time work was also said to make these students less committed to school and more involved in delinquency, truancy, substance abuse and other misconduct. The other reason that high intensity part-time work is associated with poor academic performance is that students who are not very good in school tend to be the ones who opt for high intensity part-time employment (Staff, Schulenberg & Bachman, 2010). The type of work and the experience gained from the work will also help determine how successful combining school and work could be.

"But I am Making a Lot of Money"

If you are a young person working for the first time, you may be saying or thinking, "I am making a lot of money!" That may be true for you. However, if you are spending all that you are making on non-essential things, and if you are taking time away from your schoolwork to do this, then you are really wasting your time.

Think Carefully about the Work/Study Option

While having extra money to spend, you must think wisely about what you are accomplishing. If you are a young person contemplating part-time work, you must bear in mind the positive and the negative aspects of working while studying. Yet, for some students part- time employment is necessary for survival. If you are in this situation, try to maintain a balance between work and school.

Find a part-time job that gives you the flexibility to take extra time off when your studies demand it. Make sure that your studies are minimally impacted by your part-time work.

Chapter 23 – FOOD FOR THOUGHT

Topics and Ideas for Self-Reflection and Discussion

What are your plans for summer?

Are you going to work, travel, or volunteer?

Discussion among group members or class would provide different views on how young people see summer.

What do you think about volunteering?

"Service to others is the rent you pay for your room here on Earth." — Muhammad Ali

"Volunteers don't get paid, not because they're worthless, but because they're priceless." – Sherry Anderson

CHAPTER 23: REFERENCES AND FURTHER READING

Hovdhaugen, E. (2015). Working while studying: the impact of term-time employment on dropout rates. *Journal of Education and Work, 28*(6), 631-651.

Staff, J. & Schulenberg, J.E. (2010). Millennials and the World of Work: experiences in Paid work during Adolescence. *Journal of Business Psychology, 25,* 247-255.

Staff, J., Schulenberg, J.E. & Bachman, J.G. (2010). Adolescent work intensity, school performance, and academic engagement. *Sociology of Education, 83*(23), 183-200.

CHAPTER 24

BEING MENTALLY PREPARED FOR SCHOOL

Being prepared for school requires more than getting new clothes, shoes, stationery and bag. If you are in Junior High, this may be all that seems necessary. If you are in high school, it may require more, particularly if you had been working over the summer. It may mean either ending your employment or at least making arrangements for drastically reduced hours during the semester. If you are entering college or university for the first time, this could be a time of great anticipation, apprehension, or a mixture of both. If you are returning to college or university after the holidays, you may be concerned about the new work you have to face. If you are going back to any of these situations, especially if your last school year was not very successful, you may have a host of other feelings. Being prepared for school, regardless of the level, requires that you get yourself mentally prepared for the task ahead.

ANXIETY – NOTHING TO BE ASHAMED OF

However, if you are returning to school and you are anxiously looking forward to it, this is nothing to be ashamed of. In fact, you are ahead of the game, because you have thought about the prospect of returning, and are becoming mentally prepared for the experience. Regardless of the level of education, all students should become mentally prepared for school; if not, it will very likely take several weeks to come to terms with what is expected of you.

You would quite likely start thinking about the new friends you would meet, the new teachers or professors you would have, and the new challenges you would have to face in your courses. To build confidence, probably do some reading and reviewing before school opens, if you know some of the work you will encounter.

AS A COLLEGE OR UNIVERSITY STUDENT

As a college or university student, you may find it helpful to take the time before school opens to review some of your areas of weakness. Although you may not know the content of your courses, you have to expect to do many written assignments. If you know that you are weak in writing, you should be strengthening your writing skills, probably reviewing books on how to write essays and do analytical book reviews. After all, this is an integral part of going to college or university.

ACCEPTING THE END AND THE BEGINNING

Mental preparedness involves your awareness that whatever you may be doing now may have to stop. If you spent a very relaxing summer having fun with your friends or stayed at home, you must think of returning to a busy schedule. You would have to be up at a certain time, leave home at a specific time, get on the bus or in your car, and arrive at school at a particular time. If you have not acknowledged the changed circumstances that you would be faced with in a matter of days, you would be ill prepared to fulfill expectations. This could lead to lateness and inability to concentrate or to organize yourself and your work.

Dealing with the Challenge

If you are not mentally prepared, you could find school is a real challenge. High school students would be seriously challenged if they forgot much of what they knew over the holidays. These students may need some review before going forward. Some would be fortunate to receive this help from caring teachers. Some would have to do it on their own. College and university students often do not have this luxury, because they are getting into new work, and it is their responsibility to make sure that they have the prerequisite knowledge to understand what they are expected to do. More than that, if you are a college or university student, you are also expected to organize your own work, plan your schedule, and get the tasks done. If you do not work, there is no one there to call you out on it. You will see the effects in your final grade.

Mental Preparation Covers Many Areas

Therefore, if you are a student preparing to go back to school after the summer holidays, you should pay special attention to becoming mentally prepared. Mental preparation should involve more than putting a wardrobe together and buying your books and other materials. It would involve setting up schedules if you have already received your timetables from school. If you haven't, there is still no excuse. You should plan the number of hours a week you will spend studying, that is, outside of the number of hours in class. If you do part-time work, take a careful look at what your employer expects of you, and what you expect of yourself. In short, realize that you have to change your schedule to go back to school. Know your priorities, and plan accordingly.

CHAPTER 24 – FOOD FOR THOUGHT

TOPICS AND IDEAS FOR SELF-REFLECTION AND DISCUSSION

When undertaking any endeavor, it is important to be mentally prepared. This goes for school as well. Being mentally prepared involves having the mindset to do whatever it takes to adjust well to your new environment.

Are you mentally prepared for whatever your undertaking is?

If not, what will it take for you to become mentally prepared?

"If you're trying to achieve, there will be roadblocks. I've had them; everybody has had them. But obstacles don't have to stop you. If you run into a wall, don't turn around and give up. Figure out how to climb it, go through it, or work around it." – Michael Jordan

CHAPTER 25

DON'T BE CAUGHT UNPREPARED!

When 16-year old Daphne complained that her teacher gave a surprise quiz, and she failed it, her father was not sympathetic. "You should have been prepared!"

"But she didn't tell us we were going to have a quiz," Daphne insisted.

"But she doesn't have to. You should be prepared!"

BE PREPARED

"Be Prepared!" This is the motto I learned as a Girl Guide, and that I taught to young guides as a guide leader some years ago. It is also a motto I find appropriate for students of all ages. As a student, being prepared means being ready to be tested or quizzed at any time.

IS BEING PREPARED UNREALISTIC?

I have had this conversation with some of my students who believed at one time that being prepared was unrealistic. However, after following a few simple rules, they agreed that it was not difficult at all. Here are the rules.

RULE 1: REVIEW YOUR WORK EACH DAY.

This is a practice that many students use. Reviewing what you learned each day does not have to take several hours of studying. Fifteen minutes, half an hour, or sometimes an hour, is all that may be needed. If you have more time, spend more time.

Rule 2: Take Good Notes

If you are in the higher grades or in university, this is imperative. One of the problems that some students encounter in reviewing their work is that they did not take good notes. Some students who have good memories take very limited notes: they put down only key words. Sometimes key words are all that is needed for them to link the ideas. Other students write copiously and need to do so. In either case, take notes that would help you to remember what was taught and that would aid in your better understanding of the topic.

Rule 3: Stop Writing and Listen

If you write a lot, you must be aware of a possible drawback here. You must be able to concentrate and understand what the teacher is saying in order to write the ideas in your own words. If you try to copy exactly what the teacher is saying – word for word – and you don't understand the topic, you are wasting your time. You would soon find out that although you may have copied most of what the teacher had said, your notes do not make sense.

Rule 4: Ask Questions

If you realize that you do not understand a topic, it may be possible to ask a question at this point. If you are in a lecture, this may be impossible at the time. Yet, you should seek help by speaking to your teacher later. If you are at university, you may seek help not only from your professor, but also from the teaching assistant (T.A.) that is assigned to your course. You may team up with a classmate who understands the topic and who would enjoy expanding on his or her knowledge by explaining the topic to you.

Or you could find a tutor who could help you understand the work. Your best starting point, though, is to reread the material that was assigned to you. There are times when it is necessary to read an article or assignment several times before it becomes clear.

RULE 5: READ THROUGH NOTES

If you made good notes, read them through when you get home, especially if you found a concept somewhat difficult to understand in the first place. By reading through your notes, you'd find that the concept could become clearer. If you understood the concept when it was taught, reading and rereading could only improve your understanding of it.

RULE 6: REWRITE AND EXPAND

As a student at all levels, I usually rewrote my notes. While rewriting allowed me to keep my notes neatly organized, it also helped me to understand and remember the topic. It was also at this point that I would expand on a concept by finding more information on it, usually from my text. I would include the additional information in my notes. Over the years, I have encouraged my students to do the same, and for those who followed the advice, the payoff was well worth it.

RULE 7: SO, BE PREPARED!

If you review your work on a daily basis, particularly for the subjects you find challenging, you would not be caught unprepared as Daphne was. If you follow these steps for all of your subjects, you would be ahead of the game!

CHAPTER 25 – FOOD FOR THOUGHT

TOPICS AND IDEAS FOR SELF-REFLECTION AND DISCUSSION

How to prepare to be successful in school?

Go back to this chapter and make a list of all the strategies noted here.

Also add a few strategies that you believe will work for you.

Remember:

"The expert in anything was once a beginner." — Helen Hayes

CHAPTER 26

IT'S TIME TO 'BUCKLE DOWN'

If this is your final year in high school and you are hoping to enter university in the coming year, you already know you have to 'buckle down' to some serious work. If you are in university at the present time, you also know that it is time to 'buckle down' and get all those assignments handed in. In short, it is exam time as well as the time for you to submit those papers. Get the papers out of the way, so you could put in more time and give your full attention to preparing for your exams or tests.

CUT DOWN ON UNNECESSARY ACTIVITIES

If you are feeling a little overwhelmed at this time, maybe you have lots of schoolwork to do and you do not know where to start. First, take a deep breath, and tell yourself, "I'm going to 'buckle down' and get things done." Make it a commitment and look for places where you can save time. This means you may have to forget about talking on the phone for an hour at a time. Cut down the talk to 5 or 10 minutes. This means you would have saved at least an extra 50 minutes there. Maybe you watch TV for an hour and a half or two hours as a rule, and you never thought that this was time you could use more effectively. If you have to, look at half an hour of TV to relax, if that's your excuse. Look for other places where you are spending time that you could cut back.

PRIORITIZE YOUR WORK

Prioritize your work. Which is most pressing? Do you have a test coming up for which you need to revise? Do you have papers you have to do and readings you have to catch up on? Again, before you start feeling overwhelmed, make a list of these tasks, putting the most important or the most critical ones at the top of the list. Number the tasks in order of importance. Now, make up a chart showing the hours you have available or that you would make available to study. Assign hours that you would use for the different tasks, making sure that you give more time to the tasks that require more effort and less time to those tasks that you consider not very important or that you could accomplish quite easily.

DIVERSIFY YOUR ACTIVITIES

Remember, in setting up your hours of study, diversify the things that you will be doing. For example, maybe allocating three consecutive hours to studying one subject may not be the most efficient use of time. Or if you do, break up the time into sections. If you have two or three hours to study, for optimum learning break down this time into 25-minute segments, for example. If students retain more at the beginning and the ending of each 25 minutes, as researchers have proven, then you would learn much more over the two or three hours if you study in 25-minute segments rather than if you studied non-stop for the same two or three hours.

STUDY WITH PURPOSE

Another technique to getting more efficient use of your study time is to study with a purpose. Organize your material. Don't just read everything altogether. Break down your material according to topic, and study each topic as a unit. In this way, if you were asked a question on a topic, you would be better prepared to answer it correctly.

OVER-LEARN YOUR MATERIAL

Still yet, another technique is to over-learn your material. Although you may know a topic, re-read it a few times. You would know it so well that you would be able to answer any question on it, regardless of how the question is phrased. You may even find it useful when reading your material to formulate possible questions that may be asked. In so doing, you would have explored the possible ways that you may be tested on your material. Also, if you find a technique that works best for you, use it! You are a unique individual and a unique learner, so find your easy ways of learning and take advantage of these.

DON'T BE DISTRACTED

Keep on track. Let nothing cause you to deviate from your study schedule, for you must realize that if you plan your time efficiently, there is really no time to waste. Buckle down and make sure you follow your schedule, and that you use techniques that would best help you complete your work.

CHAPTER 26 – FOOD FOR THOUGHT

TOPICS AND IDEAS FOR SELF-REFLECTION AND DISCUSSION

How do you really settle down to study and perform better in your school work?

Make a list of all the strategies mentioned in this chapter. Make the list your own by adding other strategies you believe will work for you.

Have you ever considered forming study groups within your group or class, and if you have, what has been your experience?

CHAPTER 27

IS IT YOUR LAST YEAR BEFORE GRADUATION?

During the last school year before graduation, many young people feel extra stress as they consider upcoming exams. For some, the stress is the usual, based on the uncertainty over what materials exams would cover. For others, the stress is greater, since performance on these exams could determine whether they graduate, or whether the offer for admission to their favorite university would be confirmed or rescinded, based on their final marks. Younger students could also be experiencing stress if their performance this last term will determine whether they pass or fail the grade. I have found that during this period many students experience a high level of stress and much anxiety.

MAINTAIN CALMNESS

Regardless of which student you are, this last term may be the home stretch that you dread. However, this is not the time to panic and give up because you feel stressed. This is the time to redouble your efforts, identify areas of weakness, target these areas, and determine to be successful. It is also the time to remind yourself that for peak performance you need to maintain calmness.

REDOUBLE YOUR EFFORTS

Redoubling your efforts may involve spending more time revising your work. Maybe you are good in English, but poor in Math, or vice versa.

IS IT YOUR LAST YEAR BEFORE GRADUATION?

If you are in university, you may find Political Science a breeze, but you may be struggling with the many theories in Social Psychology that you have to understand for your exam. You may be doing well in some subjects, but not in others. You may enjoy doing the subjects you excel in, but may put off working on the subjects in which you are weak. However, this is the time to identify the areas or the concepts that cause you the most difficulty. Maybe you didn't understand some earlier concepts, or maybe you forgot them. This is the time to revisit these areas, with the determination that you will learn them well and be prepared for your exam.

KNOW WHAT YOUR EXAM WILL COVER

Your next step is to find out what areas you will be tested on and make sure you know these areas well. Your teacher or professor would very likely tell the class what concepts or areas of study would be on the exams. If your teacher or professor does not give this information, ask. Or maybe study sheets have already been provided. Take these seriously, and make sure you know all the concepts presented. If you did not receive a guideline, do not be disheartened. Simply go through the material you studied, and ask yourself likely questions to ensure you know the work.

GET A TUTOR

At the high school level, if you have difficulty understanding or recalling material, ask your teacher. This should be your starting point in getting assistance. You could also get valuable help from your parents, who may be willing to sit with you and explain some of the concepts.

If your parents do not have the patience or the time, maybe they would look for other assistance for you. If you get outside assistance, make the best use of it. Ask your tutor for help in specific areas where you are likely to be tested and where you may need help. Target the concept areas where you need to improve.

TAKE RESPONSIBILITY FOR MATERIAL

You must also take responsibility for covering the material. Regardless of the help you receive, you must determine to learn and be able to perform well on your exams. This means thinking of possible questions that you may be asked, then writing out the answers to the questions. Review the questions and answers, making sure you cover all parts of the questions. Remember this when you are assigned questions on your exams. If you do only part of a question, you will only receive part of the marks for the question, even though the part that you did was perfect.

PANIC DISAPPEARS WITH GREATER CONFIDENCE

The more you become proficient in the areas in which you are weak, the greater your confidence will grow. With increased confidence, you would find that your panic disappears because you know you are capable of answering any questions that would be asked. Therefore, make this home stretch count for you. To prepare for your exams strengthen weak areas and see your confidence grow.

CHAPTER 27 – FOOD FOR THOUGHT

TOPICS AND IDEAS FOR SELF-REFLECTION AND DISCUSSION

Your last year before graduation could be very challenging. This is a common experience, as people often fear that if they did not pass their final exams that their years of study would be in vain. But this last year doesn't need to be challenging. Once you do your work consistently and complete preparation for your exams or tests, you can have confidence that you have done your best.

Here are a few pieces of advice. These could also be the basis for discussions and could lead to even more ideas on how to work and still relax.

"Don't stress. Do your best. Forget the rest." – Anonymous

"Learning is a treasure that will follow its owner everywhere." – Chinese Proverb

CHAPTER 28

YOU PROBABLY STUDIED TOO MUCH!!

"You're supposed to be graduating this year, and you're failing English?" Shawna's mother criticized, as she browsed through her daughter's notebook that was inadvertently left lying on the table.

"Failing English? What do you mean 'failing English'?" Shawna's father joined in, rushing down the stairs on his way to work.

"It was only a small test. Don't sweat it!" Shawna shrugged.

"You didn't study again?" her father nagged.

"Yes, I did!" Shawna insisted.

"And how come you failed?" her mother enquired.

"I studied. I stayed up all night before the test and read the silly book." Shawna tried to convince her parents, but in vain.

Then, there was Patrick. He completed first year at university, with his highest mark being a C-.

"You are wasting time, boy," his mother scolded.

"Why don't you study and forget about the parties and the girls," his father bellowed.

YOU PROBABLY STUDIED TOO MUCH!!

"Dad, I studied. I didn't even go out during exam time. I studied all weekend, and I still didn't get a good mark."

Shawna and Patrick studied as they said they did. However, they probably made a few mistakes in how they studied. Here are some pointers to overcome some of these common mistakes.

TRYING TO DO EVERYTHING THE NIGHT BEFORE?

First, Shawna probably stayed up all night reading a novel she should have read before. This left her no time to revise her other work. If only one of the ten questions asked on the test was based on the novel she read the night before, then Shawna was not prepared for the rest of her test.

STARTING TOO LATE

Second, Shawna probably didn't start preparing for the test until the night before. With so much to do in so little time, she could have become anxious. She could have lost confidence in herself. The result? During the test, she could have forgotten what she already knew.

BREAKING UP STUDY TIME HELPS

Third, Patrick studied all weekend before his exams. He probably studied too much. The way he studied might not have helped, either. Research has shown that people learn in bursts. When you first start studying, you retain much of what you read then. Similarly, when you stop studying, you retain much of what you learned last. Therefore, breaking up study time would seem to be the most efficient and effective way to accomplish optimum learning.

So, for goodness' sake, don't sit for hours studying non-stop. You may be actually wasting time and frustrating yourself.

ORGANIZE ACCORDING TO TOPIC

Fourth, when you study, organize your material according to topic. For example, if you were studying biology and were to be tested on the human body, by organizing the material according to the different systems in the body, you may be preparing yourself very effectively for your exam. Knowing how the systems interact and work for the functioning of the body as a whole may also be a good way of preparing for one or more of the questions on the exam.

STUDY CONSISTENTLY

Fifth, study consistently over time. Shawna and Patrick should have been studying all through the year. Had they done this, they would have had only to revise before their test and exam.

STUDY SMART

Therefore, it is important to study and study smart. It means using all those strategies available to make the most out of your study time. One of the most effective strategies is to break up your study time and organize the material that you study for better understanding. Also, anticipate the questions that would be asked and prepare for them. Then, relax and get a good night's sleep before your test or exam. Try these tips and see the difference!!

CHAPTER 28 – FOOD FOR THOUGHT

TOPICS AND IDEAS FOR SELF-REFLECTION AND DISCUSSION

Make a list of the tips that were provided in this chapter.

You may also add your own tips that you believe have helped you in studying more effectively or which you intend to use to help you in the near future.

"There are no secrets to success. It is the result of preparation, hard work, and learning from failure." – Colin Powell

CHAPTER 28: REFERENCES AND FURTHER READING

Farrow, D. (January 31, 2017). Focus bursts: Using interval training and controlled panic for better study. CampusTalkBlog. Available at
http://www.campustalkblog.com/focus-bursts/

Morrison, N. (May 30, 2016). The secret of effective learning may be less studying, not more. Available at
https://www.forbes.com/sites/nickmorrison/2016/05/30/the-secret-of-effective-learning-may-be-less-study-not-more/#69fe392118c7

CHAPTER 29

MATCHING YOUR CAREER TO THE JOB MARKET

You are graduating from high school, from college, from university, or from a vocational program. You believe you are qualified for the position that you want, or for the career you intend to follow. If you believe you have all the qualifications and skills you need for the position or the job you want, then the next step is to check out the job market that you wish to enter. Some of you may have acquired skills for which you need to find a job, while others may have developed skills that enable you to set up your own business. Regardless of the path you decide to follow, check out the job market to see what is available and what your best prospects are. You are anxious, for it is only a month left before graduation and you are thinking about your next step. You may have decided that it is time to start acting as though you have already graduated.

CONVINCING RESUME

At one time, looking for a job entailed printing out literally hundreds of resumes and sending them out to all possible employers. This approach has proven to be ineffective, with many other individuals doing the same thing. More than that, having one resume to send to every job does not really allow you to target specific jobs that are looking for specific skills.

A word of advice is to identify a specific job, target that job with a resume outlining the skills that are pertinent to the particular job, and convince the prospective employer that you are the best candidate for the job.

No Room for Errors

Here's a word of caution about your resume. Make sure that it is properly written. It is just as important to ensure that your resume does not contain grammatical and spelling errors. Nothing is more distracting as having a resume where there are spelling errors. Errors show that you are not really very careful or even "detailed oriented" as you may have written in your resume. Pay attention to possible errors in your resume. Besides being clearly written, well organized, free of spelling and grammatical errors, your resume should focus on your achievements, with the most important information about your qualifications and skills on the very first page. Your resume should not be long, and should generally be about two pages in length.

Well-written Cover Letter

Your resume should also be accompanied by a well-written cover letter, properly addressed to the contact person of the organization and clearly outlining why you are interested in the organization. Research should provide meaningful reasons for your interest in the organization. In responding to the specific position, you should demonstrate that you understand what skills and expertise the organization is looking for, and point out the strong match with your skills and expertise.

Postings on Job Sites

While contacting organizations with your resume and cover letter is a well-known approach, there are many other innovative means of reaching employers, or of having employers select you. There are many job posting sites to which you can post your jobs.

SOCIAL MEDIA - LINKEDIN

However, using social media is one of the more effective means, with LinkedIn considered the most effective. On social media, you have to show the prospective employer that you are passionate about your field, confident in your abilities, and able to make a difference in the organization in which you are hired. You have to 'show' rather than just 'tell'. A good profile could make the difference between finding a job and not finding one.

BE SENSIBLE IN YOUR USE OF SOCIAL MEDIA

On the subject of social media, Facebook is also used. But even if you do not use Facebook as a means of looking for a job, it is also a source for information about you. Prospective employers often do a social media check on candidates they are considering for employment. Your Facebook pages, if available to public viewing, can become part of your profile that may be considered with your job application or with your LinkedIn profile.

BEWARE OF WHAT YOU POST ON SOCIAL MEDIA SITES

Because of this, as a young person, you should be careful about what you post on social media sites, because these postings can come back to haunt you.

One recommendation is to check your privacy settings on Facebook and other sites, if you believe there is anything there that may compromise you. A good rule of thumb is to be careful about what you post there, for what is done and said on these sites could affect you professionally.

JOB SEARCH IS A FULL –TIME ACTIVITY

From speaking to graduates who have done, or are still doing, job searches, I discovered that it is a full-time activity on its own. Take your job search very seriously. Job search is an important activity that you cannot leave to chance. Get as much up-to-date information on how to go about doing a job search and learn cutting-edge techniques on how to make your resume more responsive and your interviews more effective. However, while you are thinking of how to go about finding a job, a few words of advice are in order.

You have to be creative and stand out from the crowd. You have to be persistent and allow the prospective employer to see you as the employee that he or she would be fortunate to have.

Chapter 29 – Food for Thought

Topics and Ideas for Self-Reflection and Discussion

Planning your career can be very challenging, especially if you do not know what you want to do.

Whatever you choose, remember you will be spending most of your waking day doing it. If you choose a job that you don't like, this will mean that for several hours a day you will be doing something you prefer not to be doing.

Consider the following quotes. You may find these are good topics for discussion among friends and in a class setting.

"Choose a job you love, and you will never have to work a day in your life." – Confucius

"Find out what you like doing best and get someone to pay you for doing it." – Katherine Whitehorn

Chapter 29: References and Further Reading

Leadem, E. (July 8, 2018). Trade School vs. College: Which is right for you? (Infographic). Entrepreneur Magazine. Available at *https://www.entrepreneur.com/article/316320*

Chapter 30

CARPE DIEM: ADVICE TO THE GRADUATING CLASS

At a recent graduation ceremony, the keynote speaker took as his topic, "Carpe Diem", a Latin phrase popularized in the movie, *Dead Poets Society*, and meaning, "Seize the day". He addressed the students and challenged them with the command, "Carpe Diem". In short, they were to 'seize the day', 'grasp the opportunity', 'face the moment' and 'engage the day'. What this means is to take advantage of the opportunities that are at hand right now. The speaker encouraged students not to wait for opportunities to come to them, but to look at what is before them and create their own opportunities.

FIND YOUR PURPOSE

The first task for the young person is to "find your purpose", or discover your purpose for living. This means looking forward to what is ahead, and determining what you are to do with your life. Expanding on this theme, I would say, try to discover what you want to do with the rest of your life, where you want to be, what you want to accomplish, and be ever cognizant of your contribution to the well-being of others. In order to do this, you have to follow a few steps.

HAVE A DREAM

You must have a dream, for "every success must begin with a dream." Without a dream, there is no purpose, because there is nothing to motivate you to set a goal. Without a dream, you will be like a ship with no destination.

A ship would not get out of the harbor if it has nowhere to go, and if it does set out from the harbor at all, without a destination, it would only flounder in the waves of uncertainty (Napoleon Hill and Clement Stone). Therefore, have a dream - have a purpose.

SOMETHING YOU WANT TO ACHIEVE

It is important to recognize that your dream does not have to be a lofty idea or a grandiose scheme, but it has to be something that you want to achieve, something you want so badly that you think about it most of the time.

FORGET THE GOOD

To achieve your dream and find your purpose, there are further steps that you should follow. Forget the past. Forget the good as well as the bad. Why forget the good? The keynote speaker encouraged the students to move beyond the past, because when you live in the past, when you continually savor the good things that happened to you, then you could be holding yourself back. Since you keep basking in past successes and achievements, you feel content that you have achieved. In this way, there is no time to create new successes and achievements because you are preoccupied with recalling the past glory and successes.

FORGET THE BAD

Why forget the bad? The same reason holds true, for when you persist in thinking about the bad things that may have happened to you, you would continually feel sorry for yourself. This is counter-productive and would only hold you back. The advice to you is to "move on with your life", and so "the past cannot hurt you anymore."

BE LIKE THE BUTTERFLY

Moving on with your life is not going to be an easy task. In fact, it could be quite a struggle, yet it is a necessary part of making your way. A good example of embracing the struggle can be seen in the case of the butterfly. Think about this story. A man who was so distressed over the struggle of a pupa to emerge into a beautiful butterfly decided to help the creature. He took a pair of scissors and with a snippet made it possible for the butterfly to emerge without the great struggle that usually takes place. To his dismay, what emerged was a butterfly with an insufficiently formed pair of wings. The butterfly died, because it needed the struggle to make its wings grow strong enough for survival.

STRUGGLE NECESSARY FOR MATURITY

Applying this analogy to yourself as a young person, you must recognize the significance of the struggle for maturity and further development. Young people must appreciatively embrace the struggle, for it is their means of survival. This also means coming face to face with opportunity.

BE DILIGENT! BE VIGILANT!

To be able to recognize opportunity, you must be diligent and vigilant. As a young person, you must be poised to "capture each precious opportunity," which is the "essence of living a full life".

This means paying attention to what is around you, and looking at things positively. In this way, you would more readily see opportunities in different situations.

CARPE DIEM: ADVICE TO THE GRADUATING CLASS

BE YOUR BEST

Therefore, as the keynote speaker encouraged, whether you are young or old, a recent graduate or a veteran, this advice is valuable. It encourages you to dream and find your purpose. It admonishes you to let go of the past, and to move on with your life, recognizing the great value that lies in the struggles you would face. This advice also reminds you that it is only through struggle that you will emerge stronger and ready to take advantage of the opportunities that you would then be able to recognize.

BE YOUR VERY BEST

Heed this advice and be the very best you can be. And remember how I started this book: "There is only one You, special and unique! Only You can be the Best You there is! When you strive for excellence, you do yourself proud. When you fail to try, when you just get by, you do yourself a great disservice." Strive for excellence in thought, word and deed. Think good and positive thoughts. When you speak, let your words be constructive, not destructive. Whatever you do, make it count for good, not bad. Be the very best you can be at home, in the community at large, at school, or even at work.

In striving for excellence, prepare yourself for a place in society. Acquire whatever training or education you need to be of service to yourself, your family and your community. Do yourself proud and take whatever action you need to accomplish this goal.

CHAPTER 30 – FOOD FOR THOUGHT

TOPICS AND IDEAS FOR SELF-REFLECTION AND DISCUSSION

Another important piece of advice was provided by Steve Jobs, as he gave the commencement address to the 2005 graduating class at Stanford University (Holliday, 2020). His message is as relevant today as it was then. It is to realize that life would not be easy, but be prepared to deal with what one is given and hold on to one's dream of doing great work.

As Steve Jobs advised:

"I'm pretty sure none of this would have happened if I hadn't been fired from Apple. It was awful tasting medicine, but I guess the patient needed it. Sometimes life hits you in the head with a brick. Don't lose faith. I'm convinced that the only thing that kept me going was that I loved what I did. You've got to find what you love. And that is as true for your work as it is for your lovers. Your work is going to fill a large part of your life, and the only way to be truly satisfied is to do what you believe is great work. And the only way to do great work is to love what you do. If you haven't found it yet, keep looking. Don't settle. As with all matters of the heart, you'll know when you find it. And, like any great relationship, it just gets better and better as the years roll on. So keep looking until you find it. Don't settle." (Quoted in Holliday, 2020).

Chapter 30: References and Further Reading

Jobs, S. (2005). Commencement address at Stanford University, quoted in Holliday, L. (2020). 51 Motivational Quotes for Students who Need Inspiration. Available at *https://www.goskills.com/Soft-Skills/Resources/Motivational-quotes-students*

CONCLUSION

Now that you are at the end of this book, I hope you found some ideas that can help you restart your education, if you had previously dropped out of school. If you were contemplating dropping out, I hope you found some ideas that discouraged you from doing so and provided alternative measures to help you improve your education.

The truth is, it does not matter whether you want to continue in an academic stream or in a trade or vocational field. You will find that as time goes by, you will benefit from improving your various skills. If you are a young parent or aspire to be one sometime in the future, you will undoubtedly encounter having to help your children with their school work. This can be a daunting task, if you are not well prepared.

If you are an older adult, I hope you gained something from this book and that you will share some of the ideas with your children, grandchildren, family members, students, or other young people with whom you interact on a regular basis. And remember, you can always gift a copy of this book to a younger person.

If you are a teacher, school counsellor, librarian, youth group leader, social worker, or another adult youth worker, you may be able to use topics in this book as prompts for discussion. You may also find this book useful as a gift to a young person. As I mentioned at the start of this book, fireside or online chats, dinner conversations, and class discussions are excellent opportunities for sharing some of these ideas with others.

CONCLUSION

Thanks for taking the time to read this book. Please share with others, and if you found this book helpful, help others to find it through your online reviews wherever you obtained this book. If you have ideas as to how I can improve this book, please send feedback to info@SuccessfulYouthLiving.com.

MORE READING AVAILABLE

If you found this book beneficial, you may also consider trying out some of the other books in this series at https://SuccessfulYouthLiving.com. See below or the back of this book for details. You can also read our blog at https://SuccessfulYouthLivingBlog.com

Thanks for reading!

Israelin Shockness

www.ingramcontent.com/pod-product-compliance
Lightning Source LLC
Chambersburg PA
CBHW060516100426
42743CB00009B/1334